D1561262

Giraffe Foods
Custom. Creative. Culinary.

Everything's better with
a little sauce. Enjoy!

Vanessa Seder
Author and Food Stylist

giraffefoods.com

info@giraffefoods.com

1.800.661.5788

[Secret]
SAUCES

[Secret]
SAUCES

Fresh + Modern Recipes

With Hundreds of Ideas for Elevating Everyday Dishes

Vanessa Seder

Photographs by Stacey Cramp

KYLE
BOOKS

To Katia, our miracle daughter who has brought us so much joy in life.
One day when your palate expands beyond PB&J and buttered noodles,
perhaps you'll enjoy some of these sauces and recipes.

An Hachette UK Company
www.hachette.co.uk

First published in 2017 by
Kyle Books, an imprint of Kyle Cathie Ltd
Carmelite House
50 Victoria Embankment
London EC4Y 0DZ
www.kylebooks.co.uk

ISBN: 978-1-909487-73-4

Text © 2017 Vanessa Seder | Design © 2017 Kyle Books | Photographs © 2017 Stacey Cramp

Distributed in the US by Hachette Book Group, 1290 Avenue of the Americas, 4th and 5th Floors, New York, NY 10104

Distributed in Canada by Canadian Manda Group, 664 Annette St., Toronto, Ontario, Canada M6S 2C8

Vanessa Seder is hereby identified as the author of this work in accordance with
Section 77 of the Copyright, Designs, and Patents Act 1988.

All rights reserved. No part of this work may be reproduced or utilised in any form or by any means, electronic or
mechanical, including photocopying, recording or by any information storage and retrieval system, without the prior
written permission of the publisher.

Editor: Christopher Steighner | Copy Editor: Sarah Scheffel
Designer: Jennifer S. Muller | Photographer: Stacey Cramp | Stylist: Vanessa Seder
Production: Nic Jones and Gemma John

Printed and bound in China
10 9 8 7 6 5 4 3 2

Right: The Mother Ganache, page 148

Contents

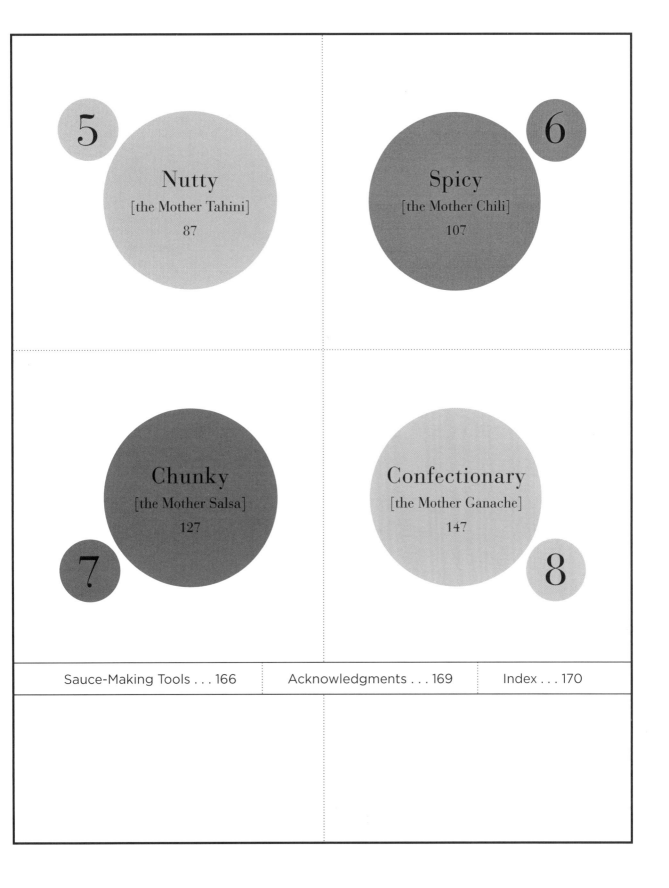

Woe to the cook whose sauces had no sting
Or who was unprepared in anything!
—Geoffrey Chaucer, *The Canterbury Tales*

Dip In

The concept for this cookbook—a collection of modern sauces with recipe pairings—was one that appealed to me for several reasons. First and foremost was the breadth of the canvas, so to speak. Sauces run the culinary gamut, spanning a multitude of cuisines, ingredients, and uses. From marinades, dressings, and dips to gravies, salsas, and curries, they can and do appear with every course, from hors d'oeuvres through dessert. Sweet or savory, hot or cold, mild or spicy, smooth or chunky, sauces encompass an endless variety of components, flavor profiles, colors, aromas, and textures.

Second, what better soapbox than a book of sauces to preach the merits of the exotic, international flavors and ingredients I love, while indulging my fascination with street foods from around the world? Plus it would allow me to draw on my culinary perspective as a born-and-bred Los Angelino and the wonderful Asian and Mexican influences prevalent throughout the city.

While I love French sauces, this book intentionally moves away from the heavy classic roux- and fond-based sauces in favor of the light, the modern, the fresh. Think miso, pistachio, avocado, and grapefruit. I have even developed my own "mother sauces"—updated alternatives to the French classics (béchamel, velouté, espagnole, tomato, and hollandaise). They're so called because each can form the base of countless variations and are designed as springboards—to act as "sauces of inspiration" you might say (sorry). I've provided three to four spinoffs for each mother, but I hope you'll experiment and create your own variants.

You'll also find evidence within these pages of the decade I lived in New York City enjoying the unbelievable ethnic cuisines hidden throughout the five boroughs. Not that I had to go far for great food; my little Brooklyn neighborhood had a wealth of really outstanding takeout options ranging from Indian, Mexican, and Thai to sushi, Middle Eastern, and more. Many of these recipes were inspired by the desire to recreate the signature sauces that came with these meals and to "decode" and reveal the secret and mysterious ingredients behind them.

Here's another secret: some sauces are hidden in plain sight. Even something as simple as seasoned olive oil can be a sauce of sorts. As you'll find, this book allows for a broad definition of what a sauce is, or can be.

I was drawn also to the idea of coming up with a featured recipe to pair with each sauce. As a chef instructor and recipe developer, I'm constantly thinking about mixing and matching flavors. However, these pairings presented a special challenge, since the purpose of any given sauce varies, depending on what it accompanies. Its role may be to enhance and intensify, to harmonize, or to provide a counterpoint to a specific dish. In some cases the sauce itself may be the star. Coming up with pairings that "worked" with each of the 65 sauces forced me to stretch my culinary muscles to their limits, requiring me to constantly refine and revise, and to draw on everything I've learned in my years of problem-solving in the kitchen.

Last but not least, as a busy working mom, I'm hyper-conscious of time and budgetary constraints, and well aware of the need to make meals family friendly. While many of these recipes feature fairly exotic ingredients, I've kept them as accessible and quick to prepare as possible, and suggested substitutes for ingredients that might be tricky to track down, or challenging for cautious palates. Many of them were tested by my neighbors, and based on their feedback I made adjustments to simplify or "kid-ify" as needed. Storage information is provided for each sauce when appropriate, along with an "Extra Credit" section with suggestions for alternative uses and repurposing.

To me the social aspect of eating and cooking is key. Delicious food transcends borders and language, and the sense of wellbeing it creates brings people together—families, friends, neighbors, and strangers alike. I hope this book will inspire you to try some new flavors and ingredients, to play around and experiment with your own sauces, and to share them with the people in your life. And it never hurts to bring along a loaf of crusty bread for dipping.

Creamy

The Mother Mayo . . . 12

The Mother Mayo

Mayonnaise is an emulsion—a mixture of two liquids that don't really like being mixed. In this case the two liquids are egg yolks and oil. When left to their own devices, these two would stay separate, but by slowly whisking the oil into the yolks, you can trick the two into forming a silky smooth sauce. The science behind this is that one of the two liquids involved acts as an emulsifier. In the case of mayo, it is the lecithin found in the egg yolks that does the job.

Makes about 1 cup

2 large egg yolks, at room temperature

1 tablespoon white wine vinegar

1 teaspoon Dijon mustard

1 cup canola or grapeseed oil

Sea salt

1. Place the egg yolks, vinegar, and mustard in the bowl of a food processor and pulse to combine. With the machine running, very, very slowly drizzle the oil into the bowl until the mixture begins to get thick and light.

2. Alternatively, you can make the mayo by hand (just be aware that this method is not as foolproof). In a large bowl, whisk together the egg yolks, vinegar, and mustard. Very slowly drizzle in the olive oil while whisking quickly until the sauce becomes thick and light.

3. Season with salt to taste. The mayonnaise will last refrigerated in an airtight container for up to 3 days.

Mix It Up

Customize the mother sauce to your taste, and to use in different ways.

Gochujang & Sesame Mayo

Stir in 2 teaspoons toasted sesame oil, 2½ teaspoons gochujang (fermented chili paste), and 1 teaspoon toasted sesame seeds.

Smoky Tomato Mayo

Stir in 2 tablespoons tomato paste, 2 teaspoons smoked paprika, and ½ teaspoon ground cumin.

Miso & Soy Mayo

Stir in 1 tablespoon sweet white miso, 1 teaspoon low-sodium soy sauce, and 2 teaspoons mirin.

Lemon & Herb Mayo

Stir in 2 teaspoons lemon zest, 2 tablespoons lemon juice, and 3 tablespoons herb of choice, such as chopped fresh parsley, chives, thyme, rosemary, chervil, or tarragon.

Extra Credit

Squiggle some gochujang or miso mayo on your **sushi**, or serve it with tempura or fried tofu.

Spread the smoky tomato mayo on a **burger** instead of ketchup.

Drizzle the miso and soy mayo over blanched **asparagus** spears.

Serve the lemon and herb mayo with any **fried seafood**, or swipe artichoke leaves through it.

AVOCADO GREEN GODDESS

Green goddess dressing, a quintessentially California invention, is typically a mixture of fresh herbs, lemon, maybe a bit of anchovy, and some creamy component. Rich and flavorful, green goddess is a simple way to add vivacity to healthy fare like poached chicken and steamed vegetables. However, it is also good on raw crunchy veggies. To make it even more California-centric, my green goddess uses avocado along with some sour cream for creaminess.

Makes about 1 cup

½ cup chopped avocado

¼ cup sour cream

3 tablespoons rice vinegar

2 teaspoons anchovy paste, optional

1 teaspoon lemon zest

2 teaspoons fresh lemon juice

½ cup chopped fresh herbs, such as flat-leaf parsley, tarragon, basil, and/or chives

Sea salt and freshly ground black pepper

Combine all ingredients in a food processor or high-powered blender and process or blend until smooth. Season to taste with salt and pepper. Use immediately or store refrigerated in an airtight container for up to 3 days.

Extra Credit

Spoon over fresh **spring greens** or Bibb lettuce; you need nothing more for a superb salad.

Drizzle the sauce over a fish, shrimp, or **lobster taco**.

Stir into shredded rotisserie chicken and place between 2 slices of bread with some baby spinach for a California riff on a **chicken salad sandwich**.

Blend with an extra avocado or two plus buttermilk to achieve a soupy consistency, then chill to create a refreshing **green summer soup**.

The Un-Crudités

Place 4 large eggs in a medium saucepan and add enough cold water to submerge the eggs by 2 inches. Bring to a boil over high heat. Turn off the heat, cover, and let steam for 4 minutes. Transfer the eggs to a large bowl of ice water until cool to the touch, then set the eggs aside.

Bring a large pot of heavily salted water to a boil over high heat. Ready a large bowl of ice water for shocking the vegetables, replacing ice as needed. Scoop ¼ cup of the avocado green goddess into a ramekin on each of four plates and set aside.

Cut 12 ounces broccoli and 12 ounces cauliflower into 3-inch florets and add to the boiling water.

Cook until crisp tender, about 4 minutes, then immediately plunge the florets into the ice water. Transfer to a colander to drain and then divide among the plates. Trim 12 ounces asparagus spears, add to the boiling water, and cook until crisp tender, about 2 minutes. Plunge them into the ice water, drain in the colander, and divide among the plates. Trim off the stem end of 10 ounces green beans, add to the boiling water, and cook until crisp tender, about 4 minutes. Plunge them into the ice water, drain in the colander, and divide among the plates.

Peel and halve the eggs and add 2 halves to each of the plates. Sprinkle with sea salt and serve immediately. **Serves 4**

HORSERADISH CRÈME FRAÎCHE

This deceptively simple sauce contributes a creamy kick to whatever it encounters, elevating even the plainest platforms, such as a skinless chicken breast. I especially like the unexpected zing it brings to any form of potato. Try it as a topping for baked potatoes, stirred into mashed potatoes, or as an alternative to ketchup for fries. Crème fraîche provides a shortcut for sauces; it gives you that unctuous texture you crave in a cream sauce but without having to make a roux with flour and cream. I recommend fresh horseradish root if you can locate it. To prepare the root, peel first, then grate with a Microplane.

Makes about 1⅓ cups

1 cup crème fraîche

3 tablespoons grated fresh or jarred horseradish

2 tablespoons Dijon mustard

4 teaspoons fresh lemon juice

Sea salt and freshly ground black pepper

Stir together the crème fraîche, horseradish, mustard, and lemon juice in a medium bowl. Season to taste with salt and pepper. Use immediately or store refrigerated in an airtight container for up to 3 days.

Extra Credit

Funnel the sauce into a squeeze bottle and use it on top of **hot dogs** or grilled sausage. It also cries out to be slathered on a roast beef sandwich.

Spoon a little on **canned sardines** or smoked oysters on saltines for a transcendent experience.

Add a dollop to **roasted beets** or on top of borscht.

For a **bagel brunch**, serve horseradish crème fraîche instead of cream cheese along with smoked fish.

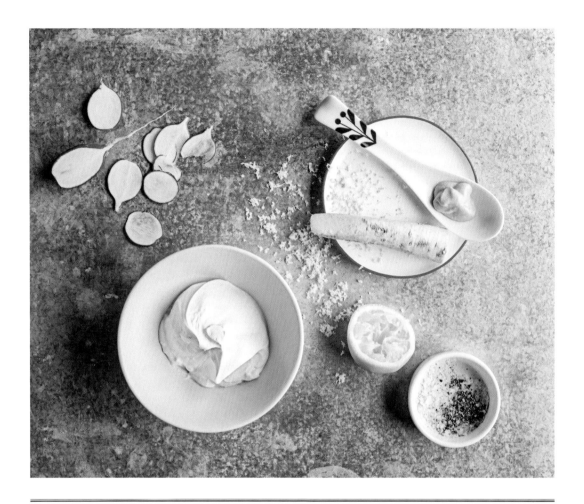

Crostini with Rib-Eye and Greens

Preheat the oven to 400°F. Cut 12 thin slices on a bias from a baguette. Place on a baking sheet and lightly brush with olive oil. Toast in the oven until lightly golden around the edges, about 10 minutes.

Heat a medium cast-iron or heavy-bottomed skillet over medium-high heat. Meanwhile, season a 12-ounce piece of beef rib-eye with salt and pepper. When the skillet is hot, coat the bottom of the pan with a bit of olive oil and add the rib-eye. Sear the steak without moving it until a brown crust

forms, 3 to 5 minutes. Flip and continue to cook the steak for about 3 minutes for medium rare, or 5 minutes for medium.

Transfer to a cutting board and let rest for about 5 minutes. Cut the rib-eye across the grain into 12 slices. Top each baguette slice with thinly sliced radishes, baby arugula, a slice of the steak, and a dollop of horseradish crème fraîche. Serve immediately. **Serves 4**

DILL AND PRESERVED LEMON RÉMOULADE

Rémoulade, a traditional French mayo-based sauce, is generally used for dipping or dressing vegetables. In Cajun cuisine, rémoulade is pink, thanks to the addition of hot sauce or cayenne pepper. I like mine more mild and fresh tasting, via the addition of Moroccan preserved lemon and fresh dill, but if it's Mardi Gras or you're craving a jolt, add a couple squirts of hot sauce.

A staple condiment of Moroccan cooking, preserved lemons could just as easily be called pickled lemons. Traditionally they are made by combining fresh lemons with large amounts of salt and lemon juice in a jar and letting the lemons pickle at room temperature. The pickling process usually takes several weeks or even longer. The peel becomes very soft and loses its pithy bitterness. Before use, many cooks wash off the salt and remove the membranes and seeds. I love preserved lemons so much I find myself eating them on their own, but they add an intense lemon flavor to any dish you choose, such as a classic tagine stew, a couscous salad, or this rémoulade.

Makes about 1¼ cups

⅓ cup sour cream

⅔ cup mayonnaise

2 tablespoons Dijon mustard

1 tablespoon finely chopped shallot

¼ cup chopped cornichons

¼ cup chopped fresh dill

3 tablespoons chopped preserved lemon

Sea salt and freshly ground black pepper

Whisk together the sour cream, mayonnaise, mustard, shallot, cornichons, dill, and preserved lemon in a medium bowl. Season to taste with salt and pepper. Use immediately or store refrigerated in an airtight container for up to 3 days.

Extra Credit

Rémoulade, especially with preserved lemons, calls out to be paired with **fish and chips** or any fried seafood.

Add some fresh lemon juice and olive oil to the mix and use as a creamy dressing over **raw baby kale**, spinach, and arugula.

Toss with **roasted carrots** and chopped fresh mint for a zingy salad.

Serve with boiled and cooled **fingerling potatoes** for an easy appetizer.

Oyster Po' Boys

Drain 16 shucked oysters in a fine-mesh sieve. Whisk together 1 large egg and 3 tablespoons buttermilk in a medium bowl. Add the oysters to the bowl and gently toss to coat with the egg mixture.

In a separate shallow bowl, whisk together 1 cup finely ground cornmeal, 1½ teaspoons seafood seasoning, ¼ cup all-purpose flour, 1 teaspoon salt, and ½ teaspoon freshly ground black pepper.

Heat 1 inch canola oil in a large high-sided skillet until it registers 350°F on a deep-fry thermometer. Dip the oysters in the cornmeal mixture and then fry in batches in the oil until golden brown and crisp, 2 to 3 minutes per batch. Transfer with a slotted spoon to a paper towel–lined baking sheet.

Slice four 8-inch rolls in half lengthwise, toast them, and spread some of the rémoulade on the bottom half of each. Top each with 4 oysters, shredded iceberg lettuce, and shredded purple cabbage. Add the top halves of the rolls and serve immediately. **Serves 4**

NYC STREET MEAT SAUCE

Nothing evokes New York City street food like the ubiquitous white sauce dispensed from clear squirt bottles at food carts from Battery Park to the Bronx Zoo. I have fond memories of the day I was first introduced to it. A recent West Coast transplant, I was temping at a large law firm in midtown Manhattan and some coworkers invited me to join them for lunch. They took me to a small cart, and as we inched closer to the front of the line, the exotic, fragrant aromas circling the air were nearly too much to take. My mouth was watering by the time I made it to the vendor. Unsure of what to order, I went with what looked like the popular choice: a simple platter of sizzling gyro meat sliced off a vertical spit, rice, salad, and white sauce. The meat was so succulent and flavorful that I was instantly hooked. But the thing that really completed the meal was that white sauce. Not quite a dressing, not quite a dip, the sauce proves to be an excellent creamy foil for smoky foods off the grill. With this recipe, you can enjoy white sauce at home, eaten from a real plate instead of a Styrofoam container. Try it at your next backyard barbecue.

Makes about 1 cup

⅔ cup whole-milk Greek yogurt

½ cup mayonnaise

1 teaspoon sugar

1 teaspoon white vinegar

1 teaspoon fresh lemon juice

1 teaspoon sea salt

In a medium bowl, whisk together the yogurt, mayonnaise, 2 tablespoons water, the sugar, vinegar, lemon juice, and sea salt until combined. Use immediately or store refrigerated in an airtight container or squeeze bottle for up to 1 week.

Extra Credit

Add a bunch of chopped fresh herbs of any variety and call it an **"herb dip"** for French fries, tater tots, or potato chips.

Liven up the blandest of cooked **chicken breasts**: run them under the broiler for a minute with some crumbled feta and this sauce.

For an easy side dish or veggie meal, top a roasted baked **sweet potato** with a few squirts of street meat sauce, some harissa sauce (page 109), fresh cilantro, and chopped almonds.

Add a bunch of chopped herbs of any variety, a tablespoon more vinegar, and 2 tablespoons olive oil to make a creamy herb salad dressing for a **spinach salad** with sliced beets and hard-boiled eggs.

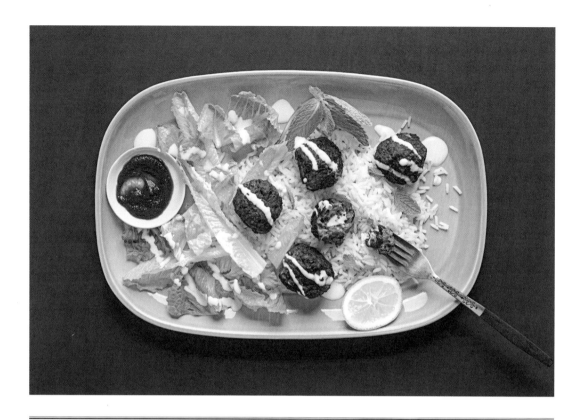

Middle Eastern Lamb Meatballs on a Bed of Rice and Greens

Preheat the oven to 200°F. Soak ¼ cup bread crumbs torn from stale bread in 2 tablespoons milk in a large bowl until the bread crumbs absorb most of the milk, about 3 minutes. Add 1¼ pounds ground lamb, 1 large egg, lightly beaten, ¼ cup chopped fresh parsley, 2 cloves finely chopped garlic, 1 teaspoon grated fresh ginger, ½ teaspoon ground cumin, 1 teaspoon ground sumac, 1 teaspoon sweet paprika, 1 teaspoon ras el hanout (Moroccan spice blend), ½ teaspoon ground coriander, ¼ teaspoon ground cardamom, 1¾ teaspoons sea salt, and ½ teaspoon freshly ground black pepper. Use your hands to mix well and shape into 16 meatballs about 1½ inches in diameter.

Heat a medium cast-iron or heavy-bottomed skillet over medium-high heat. Add 1 tablespoon olive oil to the skillet. Add half of the meatballs to the pan and cook, turning gently until all sides are browned and the meatballs are just cooked through, about 8 minutes. Transfer to a parchment-lined baking sheet and place in the oven to keep warm. Pour 1 more tablespoon olive oil into the skillet and repeat the cooking with the remaining meatballs.

Divide cooked rice among four plates. Top with the meatballs and serve with a pile of chopped romaine lettuce. Drizzle all over with NYC street meat sauce and harissa sauce (page 109), if desired. Garnish with fresh mint and a lemon wedge. **Serves 4**

SALSA GOLF

You may recognize this recipe as the "secret sauce" at old-school burger joints. But according to legend, its origins reach to Argentina. The story starts with Luis Federico Leloir, a Nobel laureate biochemist famous for his discovery and study of sugar nucleotides. Luis was something of a regular at a seaside golf resort, but he grew sick of the plain old mayo on the shrimp cocktail it served. Drawing on his chemical genius, he requested that ketchup be mixed in. And so Salsa Golf was born. My interpretation includes a bit of roasted red pepper and pickle juice, and will add a creamy charge to any number of dishes, no research required.

Makes ⅔ cup

½ cup mayonnaise

2 tablespoons ketchup

1 teaspoon fresh lemon juice

2 tablespoons chopped roasted red pepper

2 teaspoons pickle juice from a jar of dill pickles

½ teaspoon onion powder

Sea salt

Place the mayonnaise, ketchup, lemon juice, roasted red pepper, pickle juice, and onion powder in a food processor and process until smooth. Season to taste with salt.

Extra Credit

Replicate that carnival stand experience by serving some of this sauce on top of a hot dog or **sausage along with grilled peppers** and onions.

Serve alongside fries, **hash browns**, or tater tots.

Use salsa golf instead of mayo to make amped-up **deviled eggs**.

Keep it old school and nap a hunk of chilled **iceberg lettuce** with this sauce, steakhouse style.

Lobster Louie Salad

Preheat the oven to 375°F. Toss 2 cups of 1-inch Italian or white bread cubes with 3 tablespoons melted unsalted butter, 1 teaspoon Old Bay or seafood seasoning, and ¼ teaspoon salt. Spread the seasoned bread cubes out on a baking sheet and bake until golden brown and crispy, 8 to 10 minutes. Transfer the baking sheet to a wire rack to cool.

Divide 8 cups chopped romaine among four large bowls and top each bowl with one quartered hard-boiled egg, ¼ cup chopped celery, 2 tablespoons chopped celery leaves, ¼ cup chopped avocado, ¼ cup shredded carrot, ¼ cup halved small cherry or grape tomatoes, 3 ounces cooked fresh lobster meat, and the croutons. Drizzle with salsa golf. **Serves 4**

Special vs. Secret: McDonald's launched a new condiment in the 1970s, dubbing it *Special Sauce*. Not to be outdone, fast food rival Jack-in-the-Box unveiled its own take, subtly switching the name to *Secret Sauce*.

LIMEY MASALA

In the 1950s, many people emigrated from India to the UK and opened up restaurants. One evening at one such restaurant, a customer complained that his chicken tikka masala was too dry. Frustrated and insulted, the chef added a can of tomato soup and some sour cream. To his dismay, this odd hybrid masala became a hit. It is a dish hard not to love: creamy, rich, and filled with flavor from all the spices. My version of masala sauce balances the sweetness of the tomato and richness of the cream with bright notes of fresh lime and lime zest—with nary a can of soup.

Makes about 1⅔ cups

3 tablespoons ghee or butter

½ cup chopped white onion

2 teaspoons grated fresh ginger

2 medium cloves garlic, finely chopped

½ teaspoon ground cumin

½ teaspoon ground coriander

1 teaspoon garam masala (savory Indian spice blend)

¼ teaspoon fenugreek seeds

2 tablespoons tomato paste

¾ cup crushed canned tomatoes

2 tablespoons lime zest

½ cup heavy cream

3 tablespoons whole-milk Greek yogurt

1 tablespoon fresh lime juice

Sea salt and freshly ground black pepper

1. In a medium saucepan, melt the ghee over medium-high heat. Add the onion and cook, stirring occasionally, until golden, about 6 minutes. Add the ginger and garlic and cook just until fragrant, about 30 seconds, then add the cumin, coriander, garam masala, and fenugreek seeds. Stir to combine.

2. Stir in the tomato paste and cook, stirring constantly, until the tomato paste begins to caramelize, about 2 minutes. Add the crushed tomatoes, lime zest, and heavy cream and bring to a simmer, stirring constantly, until the flavors develop, 2 to 3 minutes. Stir in the yogurt and lime juice. Season to taste with salt and pepper. Use immediately or store refrigerated in an airtight container for up to 3 days.

Extra Credit

Bake **salmon** in the sauce until it flakes easily. Or, for a vegetarian alternative, try it with extra-firm tofu.

For a creamy grain or rice topping, drain a can of **chickpeas** and cook with some limey masala with handfuls of fresh spinach until the spinach wilts.

Forget those omnipresent sticky-sweet **Swedish meatballs**. Instead drape cooked meatballs in this sauce and serve with toothpicks for your next party.

New Delhi–Style Chicken Legs

In a medium bowl, stir together ½ cup whole-milk Greek yogurt and ⅔ cup cooled limey masala, 1 teaspoon ground cumin, 1 teaspoon ground coriander, 2 teaspoons salt, and 1 teaspoon pepper. Use a knife to poke holes all over 4 bone-in skin-on chicken leg quarters with the thighs still attached (about 2½ pounds total), then place them in a large resealable bag along with the sauce mixture. Remove air from the bag, seal, and use your hands to press and move the bag around to coat the chicken legs in the marinade. Refrigerate for at least 2 hours or overnight.

Preheat the oven to 425°F with racks on the middle and upper levels. Place the chicken in a single layer in a 9- by 13-inch roasting pan or baking dish. Spoon the remaining 1 cup limey masala over the chicken and use tongs to coat with the sauce. Roast on the middle rack until the juices run clear and the chicken has an internal temperature of 165°F, about 30 minutes.

Transfer the chicken to the upper rack and broil until browned in parts, about 5 minutes. Let rest at room temperature for about 10 minutes. Garnish the chicken with chopped white onion and fresh cilantro sprigs and serve alongside basmati rice and naan bread, if desired. **Serves 4**

FAUX AIOLI

Aioli has popped up on restaurant menus everywhere. It's irresistible, but if you want to make it the traditional Provençal way, you must use a mortar and pestle and include egg yolks. This widely divergent recipe skirts those items. Instead it's a simple sauce that brings together two indulgent favorites of mine: cream and tahini. Though you may think that adding cream to tahini, already rich unto itself, may seem akin to gilding the lily, each brings a different kind of richness. Plus I find that the cream and yogurt help balance any bitterness in the tahini. Some may fear using raw garlic, but take heart—this recipe doesn't call for much and it adds an intensity of flavor that you can't replicate with cooked or roasted garlic. This rich sauce is more spreadable than drizzly; if you want to thin it out, whisk in a couple tablespoons of water. I like using it in place of mayo as a spread for sandwiches.

Makes about 1 cup

¼ **cup tahini**

2 **teaspoons lemon zest**

½ **cup plain whole-milk yogurt**

2 **medium cloves garlic, minced**

¼ **cup heavy cream**

Sea salt

Whisk together the tahini, lemon zest, yogurt, garlic, and cream in a medium bowl. Season to taste with salt. Use immediately or store refrigerated in an airtight container for up to 3 days.

Extra Credit

Roast a whole **cauliflower head**, then serve with this sauce on the side for a dramatic veggie main dish.

Swirl into a bowl of **lentils** and serve with rice or couscous.

Add a dollop of faux aioli to warm broccoli, cauliflower, or **winter squash soup**.

Schmear onto toasted flatbread and fold thinly sliced roast beef or lamb on top for a **shawarma** of sorts.

Beet and Polenta Cakes

Follow package instructions to make plain coarse-grain polenta (you'll need 3½ cups cooked). Let the polenta cool to room temperature, then transfer to a large bowl.

Add 1 cup chopped roasted beets, ⅓ cup fresh chopped parsley, 1 teaspoon ground cumin, ½ teaspoon ground coriander, 2 tcaspoons fresh lemon juice, 2 teaspoons honey, 1 large egg, 1½ teaspoons salt, and ½ teaspoon freshly ground black pepper. Stir to combine and then form into 8 round cakes approximately 3 inches in diameter.

Heat 2 tablespoons olive oil in a large cast-iron skillet over medium-high heat. Add half of the cakes and cook until golden brown, about 4 minutes per side. Repeat with the remaining cakes and more oil if needed. Transfer the cakes to a plate and dollop with the faux aioli. **Serves 4**

Tangy

The Mother Vinaigrette . . . 30

The Mother Vinaigrette

Whipping up a vinaigrette is a snap. The difference between fresh and bottled is night and day, and you probably have most of the ingredients in your pantry already. Like mayo (page 12), vinaigrette is an emulsion of two liquids, but instead of oil and egg yolk, it is an emulsion of oil and vinegar. The secret is to slowly drizzle in the oil while whisking constantly to end up with a creamy and smooth texture. (Whisking, incidentally, is why even the most rotund chefs have muscular arms). Most vinaigrettes will last up to one week. They're great served with just about any green salad or grilled vegetables. I store them in jars in my fridge (just shake before use), so they're ready to make meals a snap.

Makes about ½ cup

1½ teaspoons Dijon mustard

1 tablespoon finely chopped shallot

2 tablespoons rice wine vinegar or white wine vinegar

⅓ cup extra-virgin olive oil

Salt and freshly ground black pepper

1. In a medium bowl, whisk the mustard, shallot, and vinegar together.

2. Very slowly drizzle in the olive oil while whisking constantly until emulsified. Season to taste with salt and pepper.

3. Alternatively, place the mustard, shallot, vinegar, and olive oil in a jar and vigorously shake for 30 seconds to 1 minute until combined. Season to taste with salt and pepper.

Mix It Up

Customize the mother sauce to your taste, and to use in different ways.

Tomato & Basil Vinaigrette	Parmesan & Almond Vinaigrette	Cucumber & Buttermilk Vinaigrette	Dulse & Sesame Vinaigrette
Stir in 3 tablespoons finely chopped tomato, 1 teaspoon chopped fresh oregano, and 1 tablespoon chopped fresh basil.	Stir in 3 tablespoons freshly grated Parmesan cheese, 2 tablespoons finely chopped toasted almonds, and 1 teaspoon chopped fresh thyme leaves.	Stir in ¼ cup grated peeled cucumber. Replace the vinegar with 3 tablespoons buttermilk and add 1 tablespoon chopped fresh dill.	Stir in 1 tablespoon dulse seaweed flakes, 2 teaspoons toasted sesame seeds, and 2 teaspoons toasted sesame oil.

Extra Credit

- Fill the hole of a **pitted avocado with poached shrimp** and drizzle your choice of vinaigrette over the top.

- Forget the pats of butter; Parmesan almond vinaigrette will take **baked potatoes** to a whole new level.

- Drizzle the tomato basil variation over cubes of stale bread and let sit for about 20 minutes. Then toss in fresh mozzarella, basil, and sliced tomato for an amped-up **panzanella salad**.

- Say good-bye to the powdered ranch mix that comes in a packet from the supermarket; use cucumber buttermilk vinaigrette as you would ranch dressing as a dip for carrots and/or **chicken wings**.

BENGALI SPICED YOGURT

When I was growing up in LA, my family often went to a local Indian restaurant. The food was delicious and I wanted so badly to enjoy it, but the spice level was often too much for my young palate. I felt like a wimpy kid. But then I discovered the secret power of the yogurt sauces on the side. First, there was the mild raita, filled with cooling cucumbers, and then there was the cilantro and yogurt chutney. My version is an amalgam of the two but substitutes mint for the cucumbers and cilantro. It makes a flavorful yet cooling counterpart to any dish that's laced with chile heat. With this alongside your plate, you'll never again have to worry about wimping out in the face of spicy foods.

Makes 1½ cups

2 teaspoons mustard seeds

1 teaspoon cumin seeds

1½ cups plain whole-milk yogurt

1 teaspoon grated fresh ginger

1 tablespoon finely chopped shallot

¼ cup chopped fresh mint

Sea salt

Place the mustard and cumin seeds in a medium skillet and heat over medium heat, stirring constantly until toasted, about 3 minutes. Transfer to a medium bowl. Add the yogurt and the rest of the ingredients, stir to combine, and season with salt to taste.

Toasting spices in a dry skillet or with a bit of oil intensifies their flavor. Just go easy—once the aroma hits your nose, they're done. Add to your dish or grind as needed.

Extra Credit

• Try this spiced yogurt on turkey or **lamb burgers**. Or for a vegetarian option, fried eggplant cutlets.

• Tame the spice of grilled **merguez sausages** with this cooling sauce, slathered on flatbread.

• Top a bowl full of arugula and tomatoes with a piece of **roasted salmon**. Spoon a dollop of the sauce onto the salmon for a healthy and flavorful lunch.

• Drizzle over a **grain bowl**—perhaps barley with roasted butternut squash.

Roasted Sweet Potato Wedges

Preheat the oven to 425°F. Scrub 2 large sweet potatoes (about 2 pounds worth) and slice lengthwise into ½-inch-thick wedges.

Place in a large bowl and toss with 2 tablespoons extra-virgin olive oil, 2 tablespoons brown sugar, 1 teaspoon ground cumin, ½ teaspoon ground coriander, 1 teaspoon salt, and ½ teaspoon black pepper.

Spread out on a parchment-lined baking sheet and roast, flipping once during the cooking, until golden brown and crisp in parts, 40 to 45 minutes.

Transfer to a serving dish and drizzle with Bengali-spiced yogurt. Garnish with finely chopped parsley or cilantro. Serve immediately. **Serves 4**

MISO AND LIME DRESSING

A thick fermented paste commonly made using soybeans (though it can be made with other grains or pulses such as barley or chickpeas), miso is generally associated only with the ubiquitous soup that bears its name. That's a shame, because its uses are many. For instance, in Japan it's often used as a glaze for cooked fish or eggplant; I even put it in caramel (page 162). What makes miso a standout is that it adds umami to anything it touches. Umami describes that rich and savory flavor that you get from things like Parmesan, beef broth, or mushrooms. This recipe adds a tangy citrus jolt to the mild, sweet, and salty flavor miso provides. Try it first with a mild soybean miso and then experiment with other types of miso if you like; I keep an arsenal close by at all times.

Makes about ⅔ cup

3 tablespoons sweet white miso

2 teaspoons minced garlic

1 tablespoon agave nectar or honey

1 tablespoon sesame oil

3 tablespoons fresh lime juice

1 tablespoon low-sodium soy sauce

In a medium bowl, whisk together the miso, garlic, agave, sesame oil, lime juice, soy sauce, and 3 tablespoons water. Use immediately or store refrigerated in an airtight container for up to 1 week.

Extra Credit

● Blanch **green beans** or broccoli florets and toss with the dressing. Top with sesame seeds. This side is good warm or at room temperature.

● Serve seared **tuna steak** atop salad greens with the dressing drizzled over all.

● Do a Japanese-style **potato salad** for your next picnic: toss boiled fingerlings while still warm with miso and lime dressing, and then with chopped scallions.

● Thread extra-firm **tofu cubes** and 2-inch pieces of scallions onto kebab sticks. Season with salt, brush with toasted sesame oil, and grill or broil. Drizzle with the dressing.

Seared Sea Scallops with Microgreens Salad

Remove the side-muscle from 12 dry sea scallops if you find any still attached. Season the scallops to taste with salt and pepper.

In a small bowl, toss 2 cups microgreens and 3 chopped radishes with 3 tablespoons miso and lime dressing and set aside.

Heat a cast-iron griddle or skillet over medium-high heat. Add 1 tablespoon olive oil and the scallops to the pan and cook until golden brown and seared on the outside and just opaque on the inside, about 2 minutes per side.

Divide the scallops among four plates and top each with a small mound of salad. Drizzle the scallops with additional dressing, if desired. Serve immediately. **Serves 4**

XANADU PEPPER DREAM

An exotic shiny and sweet sauce, Xanadu pepper dream was inspired by the slightly gummy, translucent red Thai sweet chili sauce I've found in local Asian supermarkets. I've always loved the addictive flavor, but wondered about the preservatives in the ingredients. So I decided to see if I could create a homemade facsimile. This version has a brighter flavor due in part to the fresh peppers. Its unctuous texture and attractive sheen come from a bit of cornstarch. From wontons to egg rolls, it's great with anything hot, crisp, and fried.

Makes about ⅔ cup

3 medium cloves garlic, crushed

2 teaspoons chopped fresh Fresno or red jalapeño chile

½ cup chopped red bell pepper

⅓ cup rice vinegar

¼ cup sugar

2 teaspoons cornstarch

Sea salt

1. Place the garlic, chile, and red bell pepper in a food processor and pulse, scraping down the bowl if necessary, until finely chopped.

2. Combine ⅓ cup water, the vinegar, and sugar in a medium saucepan and bring to a boil over high heat, 2 to 3 minutes. Stir in the garlic and chili mixture. Reduce to medium-low heat and let simmer until the garlic is soft, about 4 minutes.

3. In a small bowl, whisk the cornstarch and 2 teaspoons water until dissolved.

4. Return the sauce to a boil over medium heat. Whisk in the cornstarch and water mixture and continue to cook and stir until the sauce thickens. Continue to boil and stir for another 2 to 3 minutes. Season to taste with salt. Store refrigerated in an airtight container for up to 3 weeks.

Extra Credit

• Dab a stripe of sauce across a lettuce leaf and throw some **shredded cabbage**, carrots, scallions, and peanuts on top. Roll up and eat.

• Toss store-bought (or homemade) **fried chicken pieces** in the sauce for a sweet and crunchy treat.

• Heat a couple tablespoons canola oil in a large skillet. Add **cubed eggplant** and cook until lightly golden. Add some sauce and toss to combine. Stir in a couple handfuls of torn basil leaves. Serve with rice.

• For a party serve a platter of small **biscuits**, sliced ham, and this sauce for spreading.

Crisp Roasted Cabbage and Bacon

Preheat the oven to 400°F. Line a rimmed baking sheet with parchment paper and lay 5 slices of bacon on it. Cook until the bacon is golden brown and crisp, 18 to 20 minutes. Transfer the bacon to a cutting board and coarsely chop, reserving the bacon fat on the baking sheet.

Increase the oven temperature to 425°F. Core and slice half of a medium head of green cabbage into 1-inch-thick slices and place on the baking sheet in a single layer. Sprinkle with salt and toss in the reserved bacon fat. The leaves will separate. Return the baking sheet to the oven and roast, tossing once or twice, until browned and crisp in bits, 30 to 35 minutes.

Remove the baking sheet from the oven and add 3 tablespoons Xanadu pepper dream, tossing to combine. Return to the oven and continue to roast until the sauce caramelizes slightly, about 5 minutes. Remove from the oven and add the reserved bacon to the baking sheet. Toss to combine and transfer to a serving dish. Serve immediately. **Serves 4**

THE BLACK VINEGAR SOLUTION

If you're like me, the type of person who loves any type of Asian cuisine, it's good to have an all-purpose Asian dipping sauce recipe at your fingertips in case you suddenly need one. For example, if your local takeout restaurant forgets to slip a container in the bag with the rest of your dinner, this sauce comes together quickly and becomes a solution in more ways than one. This recipe owes its added depth to black vinegar. Originally hailing from China, black vinegar gets its distinctive flavor from the grains with which it is made—usually a combination of rice, millet, barley, and sorghum that is then fermented. You can find it in the Asian aisle at your local grocery store or Asian mart. I like to plunge everything from spring rolls, fried tofu, and of course dumplings into the inky depths of this solution.

Makes about ¾ cup

1 teaspoon raw sesame seeds

¼ cup low-sodium soy sauce

¼ cup black vinegar

½ teaspoon hot chili oil or ¼ teaspoon crushed red pepper

2 teaspoons grated fresh ginger

2 teaspoons toasted sesame oil

2 tablespoons mirin

1 tablespoon chopped fresh chives

1. Heat the sesame seeds in a small skillet over medium-low heat, stirring constantly until lightly toasted, about 5 minutes. Transfer to a medium bowl.

2. Add the soy sauce, black vinegar, chili oil, ginger, sesame oil, and mirin and whisk to combine. Stir in the chives. Use immediately or store refrigerated in an airtight container for up to 2 days. Let sit at room temperature for about 30 minutes before using.

Extra Credit

● Better than takeout: stir-fry some **leftover rice** with a scrambled egg and peas, then stir in some sauce.

● Add ⅓ cup canola oil to the black vinegar solution and shake it up to form a dressing. Try it on a Chinese-inspired salad of **celery stalks** sliced on the diagonal topped with toasted cashews.

● Sauté some chicken and vegetables (**snow peas and asparagus** are good choices), then stir in the sauce at the end for a quick Asian stir-fry.

● Boil some rice vermicelli noodles, heat them up in a pot of chicken broth, and stir in this sauce to taste. Top with cilantro, shredded carrots, chopped bok choy, and sliced chicken breast for a killer **Asian-inspired chicken soup**.

Shrimp, Watercress, and Pea Shoot Dumplings

Peel and devein ¾ pound raw shrimp. Place two thirds of the shrimp in a food processor. Coarsely chop the remaining one third shrimp on a cutting board and transfer to a medium bowl.

To the shrimp in the food processor, add 1 peeled garlic clove, 2 scallions (white and light green parts only), 2 teaspoons chopped fresh ginger, ½ cup loosely packed watercress, ½ cup pea shoots, 1 teaspoon low-sodium soy sauce, 2 teaspoons toasted sesame oil, 1 teaspoon sugar, and 1 large egg. Pulse about 20 times until finely chopped. Transfer to the medium bowl with the shrimp in it and stir in 2 tablespoons chopped scallion greens.

Ready a small bowl of water and a package of 32 dumpling wrappers. On a clean work surface, spoon about 2 teaspoons filling into the center of each wrapper. Use your finger to dab some water around the rim of the wrapper, then fold the wrapper in half and, pressing hard, crease and crimp to form a tight seam. Place on a parchment-lined baking sheet sprinkled with a bit of cornstarch. Repeat with the remaining filling and wrappers to create 32 dumplings. (You can freeze the dumplings on a baking sheet, then transfer to a sealable bag. They will keep for up to 2 months. No need to thaw before cooking as follows.)

Heat 2 tablespoons canola oil in a large cast-iron or nonstick skillet over medium-high heat. Working in batches, add 11 dumplings to the skillet and let cook undisturbed until the bottoms are golden brown and crisp, about 3 minutes. Add 2 tablespoons water to the skillet and immediately cover with a lid. Continue to cook until all the water has evaporated and the dumplings are cooked through, about 2 minutes. Transfer to a platter and serve with the black vinegar solution.

Makes 32 dumplings

When purchasing shrimp, always choose wild caught, as local as you can find it. Buy your shrimp frozen unless you know exactly when and where it was caught. What's labeled as "fresh" at the supermarket fish counters are usually brought in frozen anyway.

MAPLE BOURBON GLAZE

Here in Maine, where I've settled with my family, maple syrup is such a beloved part of the culture. There's actually a Maine Maple Sunday in March in celebration of this natural sweetener. Pure maple syrup is a labor of love that involves collecting the sap in buckets and boiling it down over wood fires. About 40 gallons of sap are needed to produce 1 gallon of syrup; hence the steep price tag. I always stash a bottle or two in the fridge to use on breakfast-related items, but I keep it in mind for savory dishes as well since the sweetness can round out spicy, salty, and rich foods. This glaze pairs maple with the smoky flavor of bourbon. It's great brushed on grilled salmon, shrimp, or chicken wings.

Makes about 3 cups

2 tablespoons extra-virgin olive oil

⅔ cup peeled and chopped shallots

1½ cups bourbon whisky

⅔ cup pure maple syrup

¼ cup Dijon mustard

¼ cup tomato paste

½ cup ketchup

2 teaspoons smoked paprika

½ teaspoon cayenne pepper

2 teaspoons apple cider vinegar

Sea salt and freshly ground black pepper

1. Heat the oil in a medium saucepan over medium heat. Add the shallots and cook, stirring occasionally, until soft, about 5 minutes.

2. Off the heat, pour in the bourbon. Raise the heat to medium-high, bring to a boil, and cook until the bourbon is reduced by half, 8 to 10 minutes.

3. Add the maple syrup, mustard, tomato paste, ketchup, smoked paprika, cayenne pepper, and ½ cup water, stir to combine, and bring to a simmer. Cook, stirring occasionally, until the flavors develop and the mixture thickens slightly, 10 to 12 minutes. Stir in the vinegar and season to taste with salt and pepper.

When cooking with spirits, wine, or beer, the goal is to extract the essence of flavor without the bite of booze. This means boiling off the alcohol, which evaporates at 172°F.

Extra Credit

- Brush the glaze on **bacon** slices, then bake until crisp; eat them like candy.

- Mix a one-to-one ratio of the sauce with water and pour enough over a pork butt to come halfway up the sides of a slow cooker. Cook for about 8 hours, until very tender. Shred the meat to make **pulled pork sandwiches** for a crowd.

- Stir some sauce to taste into **mashed sweet potatoes** for a Thanksgiving-worthy side dish.

- Make **hash brown potatoes**, stir in leftover roast beef, and drizzle with the maple bourbon glaze.

Twice-Cooked Dry-Rubbed Ribs

Preheat the oven to 300°F. Line a baking sheet with foil and top with a piece of parchment paper. Lay a 3-pound slab of baby back pork ribs meat side up on top of the parchment paper and set aside. In a small bowl, stir together 2 teaspoons regular paprika, 2 teaspoons smoked paprika, 2 teaspoons chili powder, 2 teaspoons garlic powder, 2 teaspoons onion powder, 2 tablespoons dark brown sugar, 2 teaspoons kosher salt, and 1 teaspoon black pepper. Rub the spice mixture all over the ribs. Cover the baking sheet tightly with another sheet of foil and cook for about 1 hour.

Remove from the oven and spoon ¾ cup maple bourbon glaze over the ribs. Cover and seal with foil again and return to the oven. Cook until very tender, 1½ to 2 more hours.

Preheat a grill, grill pan, or broiler. Grill or broil the ribs until crispy in parts, turning occasionally, 6 to 12 minutes total. Brush with more maple bourbon glaze, slice between the bones, and serve. **Serves 4**

WAIKIKI TERIYAKI

Teriyaki sauce is due for a reappraisal. Over the years commercial versions have turned it into a sickly sweet concoction. If you make it at home though, you can control how much sugar goes in the mix. This version exploits Hawaiian cuisine's unique blend of Polynesian and Asian-influenced flavors. Putting fresh pineapple in the mix, this riff on Hawaiian barbecue sauce makes a great marinade for meats or an accompaniment for vegetables. Try it with asparagus, sweet potatoes, or taro.

Makes about 1¾ cups

1½ cups chopped fresh pineapple

1 tablespoon canola oil

1 tablespoon chopped fresh ginger

2 medium cloves garlic, finely chopped

2 tablespoons dry sherry

½ cup low-sodium soy sauce

⅓ cup packed dark brown sugar

1. Place the pineapple in a food processor and purée until smooth, about 2 minutes.

2. Heat the canola oil in a medium saucepan over medium heat. Add the ginger and garlic and cook until fragrant, about 1 minute. Add the sherry and cook until reduced by half, about 2 minutes. Add the puréed pineapple, soy sauce, and brown sugar and cook, stirring occasionally, until heated through, about 5 minutes. Use warm, room temperature, or cold. Store refrigerated in an airtight container for up to 1 week.

Extra Credit

• Use Waikiki teriyaki in place of duck sauce to dip egg rolls, **fried wontons**, or vegetable tempura.

• Brush and baste oven-roasted **chicken wings** with this sauce for a sweet and tangy chicken appetizer.

• Cut ripe **plantains** into chunks and sauté until tender, then toss them in the pan with some of the sauce until glazed.

• Baste **pork tenderloin** with this sauce while grilling it. Slice it against the grain and spoon more sauce over the top. Serve with rice and sautéed snow peas.

Pork and Shrimp Pineapple Fried Rice

Heat 2 tablespoons canola oil in a large high-sided skillet over medium heat. Beat 2 large eggs, pour them into the pan, and swirl to spread them out. Cook without stirring until just set, about 2 minutes. Use a spatula to scrape the eggs out onto a cutting board and slice into ribbons. Set aside.

Return the skillet to the stovetop. Season ¾ pound boneless pork shoulder, trimmed and cut into ½-inch pieces, with 1½ teaspoons salt and ½ teaspoon black pepper. Increase the heat to medium-high. Add 1 tablespoon canola oil, swirl to coat the pan, then add the pork. Cook without stirring for about 2 minutes, then continue to cook, stirring once or twice, until just cooked through, about 3 minutes more.

Add ¼ cup chopped scallion (white and light green parts), 2 tablespoons finely chopped ginger, and 3 medium cloves chopped garlic and cook until fragrant, about 1 minute. Add 1 cup chopped red bell pepper, 1 cup chopped pineapple, and ½ pound peeled and deveined medium shrimp. Cook, stirring occasionally, until the shrimp are opaque and curled, 3 to 4 minutes.

Add 3 cups leftover cooked rice and toss to combine. Heat through, about 4 minutes. Stir in 2 cups packed baby spinach, ½ cup chopped scallion greens, and ½ cup Waikiki teriyaki sauce. Toss and cook until the spinach wilts, about 2 minutes. Add the eggs and gently toss. Serve immediately, garnished with chopped toasted salted cashews and lime wedges. Drizzle with additional Waikiki teriyaki sauce. **Serves 4**

GINGER CARROT FIXER

You know that salad dressing that seems mandatory in every Japanese steakhouse in America? The one with the supernatural orange color and addictive flavor you can't place? I've always loved it to the point of licking the bowl at the end of the meal (at least that's better than licking the chopsticks). This is my back-engineered version for the home. There are no oranges; the bright glow comes from raw carrots. The sesame oil is also key. It has a savoriness that makes you want to keep eating. This one is easy to whip up and keep around for drizzling on just about any salad. I call this one "the fixer" because it can take the blandest ingredient to delicious in just one swipe.

Makes about 1½ cups

3 medium carrots, peeled and cut into 1-inch chunks

2 tablespoons finely chopped fresh ginger

2 scallions, chopped, whites and light green parts only (save the dark greens for another use)

¼ cup rice vinegar

3 tablespoons mirin

2 tablespoons low-sodium soy sauce

2 teaspoons toasted sesame oil

½ cup canola or grapeseed oil

Sea salt

Place the carrots, ginger, scallions, vinegar, mirin, soy sauce, sesame oil, and canola oil in a high-speed blender or food processor. Blend until smooth. Season to taste with salt and blend to incorporate. Store refrigerated in an airtight container for up to 1 week.

Extra Credit

● Beyond salad, try this on cooked greens like **spinach or kale**—either sautéed as a warm side dish, or in the style of Japanese ohitashi appetizers (blanched, squeezed dry, and doused with the sauce).

● Add some veggies to your meat **dumplings** by using this as the dipping sauce. Or use as a dunker for chicken kebabs.

● Combine equal parts of this sauce with the mother tahini (page 88), for a killer **grain-bowl topping**.

● Place small cubes of tofu on **cucumber rounds**, drizzle with the sauce, sprinkle with finely sliced scallions, and you have a party-worthy appetizer that's especially refreshing in the warmer months.

Radish and Turnip Salad with Crispy Shiitakes

Divide 8 cups mesclun salad greens among four bowls. Use a mandoline or a sharp knife to thinly slice 4 radishes, 4 baby turnips or 1 medium peeled turnip, and one quarter of a seedless cucumber. Scatter these vegetables on top of the greens.

Peel, pit, and thinly slice 1 avocado and divide the slices among the four bowls. Top each bowl with a small handful of pea shoots.

Remove the stems from 6 ounces shiitake mushrooms and thinly slice the caps. Heat 2 tablespoons canola oil in a large skillet over medium-high heat. When hot, add half of the mushrooms to the skillet and let cook, undisturbed, until golden brown around the edges. Flip and continue to cook the mushrooms until crisp and brown, 4 to 6 minutes total. Transfer to a plate and sprinkle the mushrooms with salt to taste. Repeat with the remaining batch.

Top the salad bowls with the mushrooms and drizzle with ginger carrot fixer to taste. Serve immediately. **Serves 4**

Herby

The Mother Pesto . . . 50

The Mother Pesto

Most people associate pesto with the ubiquitous combination of basil and pine nuts—a surefire winner, yes—but it's just one of many possible combos. The truth is, if you have 1) an herb or veggie base, 2) a nut or seed, 3) some sort of hard cheese, 4) garlic or something in the allium family, 5) a touch of acid, and 6) lots of olive oil, you are in business, pesto-wise. A few caveats: always make sure to wash and dry your greens thoroughly. Season appropriately at the end and don't overly blend or crush. Toss a pesto with any pasta or use as a substitute for marinara on a pizza, slather it on an omelet, use as a sandwich spread . . . I could go on all day. In fact, pesto is just as good for breakfast as it is for dinner.

Makes about 1 cup

⅓ cup raw pine nuts

2 cups packed fresh basil leaves, thoroughly washed, dried, and torn

2 medium cloves garlic, crushed

1 teaspoon fresh lemon juice

¼ cup grated Parmesan

½ cup extra-virgin olive oil

Sea salt and freshly ground black pepper

1. Heat the pine nuts in a small skillet over medium heat while stirring constantly until lightly toasted, about 6 minutes. Immediately transfer them to the bowl of a food processor to cool.

2. Add the basil to the food processor along with the garlic, lemon juice, and cheese. Pulse about 40 times until very finely chopped. Continue to pulse while slowly drizzling in the olive oil until all the olive oil is incorporated and the pesto is smooth but slightly chunky. Season to taste with salt and pepper. Use immediately or place a piece of plastic directly over the top of the pesto so that it doesn't oxidize. Refrigerate in an airtight container for up to 3 days.

Mix It Up

Customize the mother sauce to your taste, and to use in different ways.

Carrot-Top, Kale, & Lemon Pesto

Replace the basil with 1 cup packed carrot-top leaves removed from the stems of carrots and 1 cup packed chopped kale leaves. Add 1 tablespoon lemon zest and increase the lemon juice to 2 tablespoons.

Arugula, Walnut, & Pecorino Pesto

Replace the basil with baby arugula, replace the pine nuts with raw walnuts, and replace the Parmesan with ½ cup grated pecorino cheese.

Parsley, Sun-Dried Tomato, & Cashew Pesto

Replace the basil with 1 ½ cups loosely packed chopped fresh flat-leaf parsley, add ½ cup chopped sun-dried tomatoes, and replace the pine nuts with raw cashews.

Cilantro, Pepita, & Manchego Pesto

Replace the basil with 1 ½ cups loosely packed chopped fresh cilantro, replace the pine nuts with ½ cup raw shelled pepitas, and replace the Parmesan cheese with grated mild Manchego cheese.

Extra Credit

- Thin out any of the pestos with some water and a bit of vinegar to make a divine **salad dressing**.

- Do as they do in Provence and stir pesto into a **veggie soup** (but then in this case call it pistou).

- Turn your **potato salad** super-green: Ditch the mayo, add blanched green beans, and toss everything with pesto to coat.

- Top a piece of toasted **rustic bread** with fresh mozzarella, chopped fresh tomatoes, and a spoonful of any one of the pestos. Easy Caprese!

GARLIC, LEMON, AND MINT CHIMICHURRI

An Argentinean parilla without chimichurri would be like a French fry stand without ketchup. This classic steak sauce, usually consisting of some variety of fresh herbs, aromatics, and oil, is delicious spooned over any type of grilled meat or seafood. My take on chimichurri incorporates notes of mint and lots of citrus, which lightens things up, making for a sauce versatile enough to pair with veggies, too.

Makes about 1½ cups

2 cups packed fresh flat-leaf parsley stems and leaves

1 cup loosely packed fresh mint leaves

2 tablespoons fresh lemon zest

2 medium cloves garlic, chopped

2 teaspoons brown sugar

3 tablespoons fresh lemon juice

1 cup extra-virgin olive oil

Sea salt

Pinch of crushed red pepper, optional

1. Combine the parsley, mint, lemon zest, garlic, and brown sugar in a food processor. Pulse a few times, until the herbs are coarsely chopped. With the processor running, add the lemon juice, then slowly drizzle in the olive oil in a thin stream until combined. Season to taste with salt and the crushed red pepper, if desired.

2. Use immediately or store refrigerated in an airtight container for up to 3 days.

In Argentina, *parillas*, wood-fired meat-centric restaurants, are ubiquitous. Each *parilla* has its own version of chimichurri. Legend has it chimichurri was named in honor of an Irishman named Jimmy McCurry who supported Argentina's independence in the 19th century. The locals had trouble pronouncing his name; hence *chimichurri*.

Extra Credit

- Roast a bunch of **carrot chunks** then toss them with this sauce—delicious warm or at room temperature.

- Stir into brown rice along with some fresh peas, baby spinach, and crumbled feta for a **whole-meal salad** to bring to work.

- For a summery veggie dinner, grill a lot of asparagus and some **eggplant**. Roughly chop the two, then add to pasta and toss with the chimichurri sauce.

- Steam **clams** with a little water in a covered pot until they open, stir in this sauce, and serve over fregola or couscous.

Grilled Sirloin, Potato, and Asparagus Salad

Put 1 pound small new potatoes in a medium saucepan and add enough cold water to cover by 2 inches. Bring to a boil and cook over high heat until the potatoes are tender, about 10 minutes. Drain the potatoes and cut each in half. Transfer to a large bowl with 1 bunch trimmed asparagus spears. Drizzle the potatoes and asparagus lightly with olive oil and season to taste with salt and pepper.

Preheat a grill or grill pan to medium-high heat. Add the potatoes and asparagus to the grill and cook, turning occasionally, until grill marks form and the asparagus is crisp tender. Transfer the potatoes and asparagus to four large plates or bowls. Top each with ½ cup baby arugula.

Season two 8-ounce sirloin steaks liberally with salt and pepper. Lightly oil the grill or grill pan and grill the steak for 4 to 6 minutes per side for medium (140–145°F) or 3 to 5 minutes per side for medium rare (130–135°F). Transfer the steak to a cutting board and let rest for about 5 minutes. Slice the steaks across the grain and add to the plates with the vegetables. Drizzle with chimichurri sauce. Serve warm or room temperature. **Serves 4**

SALSA VERDE FOR THE ANCHOVY-WARY

Not to be mistaken with the tomatillo-laden Mexican sauce of the same name, this classic fresh green sauce blends fresh herbs, tart citrus, and briny capers. If you can be bothered, I recommend using the authentic hand-chopping technique to preserve and heighten the delicate flavors of the herbs—but if you don't have time I won't judge you. This sauce adds life to anything from veggies (try with artichokes) and bread (especially focaccia) to seafood and steak.

While the classic version calls for anchovies, which I love, I've left them out in deference to those of you who do not. You'll still get a healthy dose of umami flavor from the capers here. But if you are anchovy friendly, try chopping up a few fillets to stir in, or use a teaspoon of anchovy paste.

Makes about ¾ cup

2 medium cloves garlic

1 teaspoon sea salt

1 teaspoon orange zest

1 teaspoon lemon zest

2 tablespoons fresh lemon juice

½ cup extra-virgin olive oil

½ cup loosely packed chopped fresh flat-leaf parsley

¼ cup loosely packed chopped fresh basil

3 tablespoons chopped fresh mint

1 tablespoon drained capers

Freshly ground black pepper

1. Place the garlic cloves on a cutting board. Using the side of a chef's knife, press to crush the garlic. Add the salt to the garlic and continue to chop and press with the side of the knife until a paste forms.

2. Transfer the salted garlic to a bowl along with the orange zest, lemon zest, lemon juice, and olive oil. Stir in the parsley, basil, mint, and capers. Season to taste with pepper. Store refrigerated for up to 2 days. Bring back to room temperature before using.

- Stir into a pot of **white beans** and serve with rustic bread for a divine meatless supper.

- Thread shrimp and **zucchini chunks** onto skewers, brush with olive oil, and grill or broil. Then paint with this sauce and serve more for dipping.

- Marinate **bocconcini** (small mozzarella balls) in this sauce for up to a day, then serve with toothpicks for a party. Yum!

- Warm a few tablespoons of olive oil over low heat. Add a couple cups of good-quality **olives** and heat through. Pour the sauce over the top and serve as a warm marinated olive appetizer.

Scallop Crudo with Citrus and Chiles

Remove the side muscles if any are still attached from ½ pound day boat or sushi-grade dry sea scallops. Slice each scallop horizontally in half and place on a large platter.

Use a sharp knife to carefully cut the top and bottom peel off of 4 oranges and 1 lime. Slice the remaining peel and pith away from the flesh and discard. Cut between the membranes to segment the oranges and lime, working over a medium bowl to catch the segments and any juices. Spoon the citrus segments and juices over the scallops.

Thinly slice 1 Anaheim or red jalapeño chile and sprinkle over the scallops. Generously drizzle the scallops with some of the salsa verde. Season to taste with salt and pepper. Serve immediately.

Serves 4

Briny capers, the signature ingredient of salsa verde, may look like tiny olives at first, but they are in fact the pickled flower buds that come from a shrub that grows wild in the Mediterranean.

THE GREAT SHALLOT AND PARSLEY CAPER

This wine and herb sauce is simple and classic, and it adds a pop of flavor to savory dishes of every stripe. Loosely inspired by the flavors of maître d'hôtel, the compound butter frequently used in French cuisine, this sauce uses as its foundation shallots, parsley, and capers plus some fresh lemon juice to brighten things up. It doesn't take long to cook and will be a welcome addition poured over vegetables like asparagus and squash, a delicate piece of fish, or even a pan-seared steak like the ones found at a French brasserie. Vive le roi!

Makes about ½ cup

1 tablespoon unsalted butter, plus 2 tablespoons cold unsalted butter, cut into small pieces

1 tablespoon extra-virgin olive oil

1 medium shallot, chopped

¼ cup dry white wine

¼ cup low-sodium chicken or vegetable broth

2 tablespoons drained capers

1 teaspoon lemon zest

1 tablespoon fresh lemon juice

3 tablespoons chopped fresh flat-leaf parsley

Sea salt and freshly ground black pepper

1. Melt 1 tablespoon of the butter with the olive oil in a medium skillet over medium heat. Add the shallot and cook until softened, about 3 minutes.

2. Add the wine and cook until reduced by half, about 3 minutes. Add the broth and capers and cook until reduced by half, about 3 minutes. Turn off the heat, stir in the lemon zest and juice, then whisk in the 2 tablespoons cold butter, a little at a time, until the sauce thickens. Stir in the fresh chopped parsley. Season lightly with salt and pepper. Serve immediately.

Extra Credit

• Drizzle on top of roasted broccoli, **Brussels sprouts**, or cauliflower for a flavorful side dish.

• Toss the sauce with pasta, along with fresh olives, arugula, and shredded **rotisserie chicken** for an easy dinner.

• Make **Caprese towers**: stack layers of sliced beefsteak tomatoes and sliced fresh mozzarella. Warm in a 350°F oven just until the cheese begins to melt. Then drizzle with the sauce and sprinkle torn fresh basil leaves on top.

• Cook skin-on **chicken breasts** in a pan until crispy and cooked through, then nap with this sauce on the plate. Serve with boiled potatoes for a bistro-worthy supper.

Eggplant Crisps

Slice 2 Italian eggplants (about 1⅓ pounds total) crosswise into ¼-inch slices. Place in a large bowl with ⅓ cup cornstarch and toss to combine and thoroughly coat.

Pour 1 inch of canola oil (about 6 cups worth) into a large pot and heat over medium-high heat until it reaches 360°F on a deep-fry thermometer. Working in batches, fry the eggplant for 3 to 4 minutes total, flipping halfway through cooking, until golden brown and crisp on both sides. If the oil starts to smoke, lower the heat. Drain off extra fat by transferring the eggplant with a slotted spoon or spider to a paper towel–lined plate. Lightly sprinkle with salt. Repeat with the remaining eggplant slices.

Transfer to a serving platter. Drizzle with the wine and herb sauce and a squeeze of fresh lemon. Serve immediately. **Serves 4**

ROASTED RED PEPPER AND OREGANO PICANTE

One reliable indicator of a good restaurant is the bread. In Brooklyn my husband and I frequented this little Italian place that brought to the table hot, chewy bread with a ramekin of what looked like tomato sauce, except it wasn't. Half good olive oil and half smashed, thickened tomatoes with hits of herbs and garlic, it was saltier and more intense than pasta sauce; we'd invariably ask for more. This is an homage with a twist: I've swapped roasted red peppers for most of the tomatoes and fresh oregano for the herb mix. Besides being a killer dipper for bread, it also works well as a condiment for meat or chicken.

Makes about 1¾ cups

2 medium red bell peppers

¼ cup extra-virgin olive oil

4 cloves garlic, thinly sliced

¼ to ¾ teaspoon crushed red pepper

1 tablespoon tomato paste

¼ cup crushed tomatoes

1 teaspoon sugar

1 tablespoon chopped fresh oregano

Sea salt and freshly ground black pepper

1. Place the peppers on a baking sheet and broil them, turning occasionally until completely charred, about 15 minutes. Transfer to a medium bowl, cover with plastic wrap, and let steam for about 10 minutes. Carefully peel and seed the peppers and finely chop them.

2. Heat the olive oil and garlic in a medium saucepan over medium-low heat. Cook, stirring occasionally, until the garlic is very soft and just beginning to turn golden, about 5 minutes. Add the crushed red pepper and tomato paste and stir to combine.

3. Stir in the roasted red pepper, crushed tomatoes, oregano, ¼ cup water, and the sugar. Raise the heat to medium, bring just to a simmer, and cook, stirring occasionally until the flavors develop, about 3 minutes. Season to taste with salt and pepper.

Extra Credit

● Swap out for tomato sauce to make a **lasagna** picante.

● Warm up some corn tortillas, spread with refried beans, cheese, shredded lettuce, corn, and chopped fresh tomatoes, then top with this sauce for perfect **veggie tacos**.

● For a Tunisian-style brunch dish, sauté sliced onion in olive oil in a cast-iron skillet. Stir in the sauce, then crack 6 to 8 **eggs** over the top. Bake at 400°F until the whites are set.

● Place rounds of **goat cheese** on crackers, then dollop with this sauce. Pair with a robust red wine.

Hot and Cold Flatbread

Stir 2¼ teaspoons (1 packet) active dry yeast and 1 tablespoon sugar into 1½ cups slightly warm (110°F) water. Let stand for 5 minutes. In a large bowl, whisk together 3 cups all-purpose flour and 2 teaspoons sea salt. Add the yeast water and 3 tablespoons olive oil and mix until a soft dough comes together. Turn the dough out onto a lightly floured work surface. Knead, adding more flour if necessary, until the dough becomes more elastic, about 3 minutes. Form the dough into a ball, transfer it to a lightly oiled large bowl, cover loosely with a piece of plastic wrap, and place on the counter. Let rise until doubled, 1 to 1½ hours.

Punch down the dough and turn it out again onto a lightly floured surface. Divide the dough into 4 equal-sized balls. Use your hands to gently stretch each piece of dough into an 8-inch diameter round.

Preheat a grill pan over medium-high heat. Brush with olive oil and add one flatbread to the pan. Cook for 8 to 10 minutes total, flipping halfway through cooking. Repeat with the remaining dough.

Spread ⅓ cup picante sauce on top of each flatbread, then top each with 3 ounces sliced fresh mozzarella and a generous handful of arugula. Drizzle with olive oil and season to taste. **Serves 4**

PURPLE BASIL AND ALMOND SMASH

Purple basil: I'll see it at the farmers' market, make a mental note to buy a bunch next time, and then miss my chance. Its growing season is relatively short. Well, last year I finally planted some and it grew like wildfire, causing my issue to go from can't get any to what do I do with it? Fortunately a saucy idea came to mind. This recipe is the result: it's great on a slew of dishes, thanks to purple basil's slightly clovelike, subtly spicy flavor and striking color. It is reminiscent of pesto, but since it has no cheese, it will still please your vegan friends. And if you miss the short seasonal window, green basil can always be substituted.

Makes about ¾ cup

2 tablespoons raw almonds

½ teaspoon sea salt

1 cup packed purple or green basil leaves

1 tablespoon lemon zest

1 tablespoon fresh lemon juice

1 to 2 teaspoons thinly sliced fresh chile pepper, such as red jalapeño

½ cup extra-virgin olive oil

In the bowl of a food processor, combine the almonds and salt and process until finely ground. Add the basil, lemon zest, lemon juice, and chile pepper and pulse until finely minced. Slowly drizzle in the olive oil while pulsing to combine. Serve immediately.

Extra Credit

- Toss cold shredded **chicken breast** with capers and cooked and cooled new potatoes, then drizzle with the sauce for a great picnic salad.

- Roll **roasted corn** on the cob through this sauce for extra crunch and color. Yum!

- Dip raw **peppers** and/or fennel into this sauce.

- Sprinkle sliced **peaches or nectarines** in coupe glasses with this sauce (omit the chile, if you prefer) for an elegant palate cleanser or a light summer dessert.

Blueberry Caprese Open-Faced Sandwiches

Preheat the oven to 375°F. Place 4 slices of dark rye bread on a baking sheet and drizzle each with 2 teaspoons olive oil. Toast in the oven until just beginning to crisp, 6 to 8 minutes. Divide the bread among four plates.

Layer each slice of toast with 2 slices prosciutto, 2 ounces Burrata or buffalo mozzarella cheese, ¼ cup arugula, 2 tablespoons microgreens, some basil leaves, and ¼ cup halved blueberries. Drizzle with the purple basil and almond smash. Serve immediately. **Serves 4**

Thai basil and lemon basil are just the tip of the iceherb— sorry, iceberg. Check farmers' markets or seed catalogs to grow your own; there are more than forty varieties from which to choose.

THYME GRAPEFRUIT BEURRE BLANC

I like to think of myself as a super smeller or, more elegantly put, an olfactory wizard. For better or worse, I can't help noticing smells, of any kind, and commenting on them—a habit, I've come to realize, that may annoy the less nasally inclined. In any event, this sauce is good for those like me who are keen to scents. It is equally pleasing to the nose and the taste buds. Slightly sweet, tart, and herby, this feels like summer in a pot. It is a great addition to foods that are light or bland, such as steamed vegetables or chicken breast. The aromatherapy qualities are an added benefit.

Makes about ¾ cup

1 tablespoon ruby red or yellow grapefruit zest

1¼ cups fresh ruby red or yellow grapefruit juice (from 2 to 3 grapefruits)

3 tablespoons honey

1 sprig thyme, plus 1 teaspoon chopped fresh thyme leaves

2 teaspoons extra-virgin olive oil

3 tablespoons cold unsalted butter, cut into small pieces

Sea salt and freshly ground black pepper

1. In a medium saucepan, combine the grapefruit zest, grapefruit juice, honey, thyme sprig, and olive oil. Bring to a boil over high heat and cook until reduced by half, 6 to 8 minutes.

2. Turn off the heat and stir in the chopped thyme, then whisk in the butter, a little at a time, until thickened. Season to taste with salt and pepper. Remove the thyme sprig, and blend with an immersion blender or whisk until frothy. Serve warm or room temperature.

Extra Credit

• Drizzle over pan-seared scallops, salmon, **mild white fish**, or even lobster.

• Spoon over steamed **green beans**, then top with crunchy toasted almonds and bread crumbs for a winning side dish.

• Use thyme and grapefruit beurre blanc as a dipper for **coconut-crusted shrimp** or chicken breast.

• Roast leeks or **spring onions** until charred in spots (as they do in Catalonia), then drizzle this sauce on top.

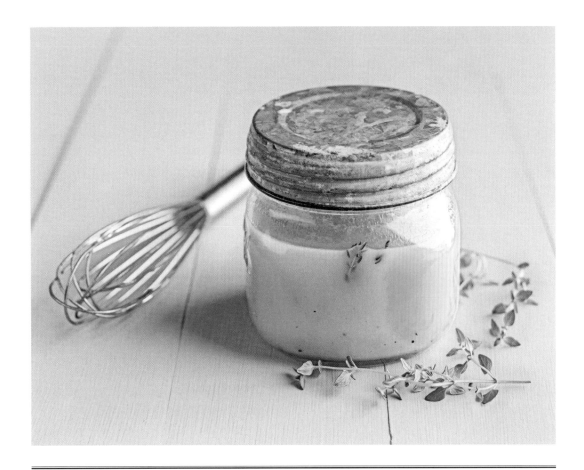

Grilled Shrimp with Fennel and Avocado Salad

Place ½ pound peeled and deveined large shrimp in a medium bowl with 1 teaspoon salt, ½ teaspoon black pepper, and 1 tablespoon olive oil. Toss to combine.

Meanwhile, use a sharp knife to carefully cut the top and bottom peel off 2 ruby red grapefruits. Slice the remaining peel and pith away from the flesh and discard. Cut between the membranes to segment the grapefruits over a medium bowl to catch the segments and any juices.

Trim the bottom and cut the fronds off 1 large bulb of fennel. Reserve ½ cup fronds. Thinly slice the fennel and add to the bowl with the grapefruit. Halve, pit, and chop 1 avocado and add to the bowl. Season to taste with salt and pepper and toss to combine.

Divide the salad among four plates. Preheat a grill or grill pan to medium heat and grill the shrimp 2 to 3 minutes per side, or until cooked through and curled. Top each salad with some shrimp. Drizzle each plate with the grapefruit beurre blanc. Serve immediately. **Serves 4**

HERBED BROWN BUTTER

Browned butter seems to be popping up all over the place these days at restaurants and in people's kitchens, but if you're like me, or pretty much anybody else, you never tire of it. The magic happens when you cook butter past the stage of just melted, until the milk solids float up to the top and begin to caramelize, at which point the butter turns from golden yellow to golden brown. The aroma at this stage will go from creamy to nutty, as will the flavor. By itself, brown butter can be added to just about anything from meat, fish, and vegetables to desserts. Here I've added fresh herbs to balance out the richness with a hit of fresh green flavor.

Makes about ¼ cup

4 tablespoons (½ stick) unsalted butter

1 teaspoon finely chopped fresh flat-leaf parsley

1 teaspoon finely chopped fresh sage

1 teaspoon finely chopped fresh thyme leaves

½ teaspoon finely chopped fresh rosemary leaves

Sea salt and freshly ground black pepper

In a small saucepan, heat the butter over medium heat until it has melted, about 4 minutes. Continue to cook without stirring until the butter has a nutty aroma and the milk solids begin to turn golden brown around the edges, 3 to 4 minutes more. Turn off the heat and immediately stir in the herbs and season to taste with salt and pepper. Serve right away.

Extra Credit

• Stir herbed brown butter into **rice or couscous** with some chopped toasted almonds for a divine pilaf.

• Give **turkey leftovers** a second chance by drizzling them with this sauce.

• Make **savory crepes** (or Italian-style crespelle), roll them around a filling of a soft cheese like ricotta, then drape them with this sauce for a decadent brunch offering.

• Toss with **ravioli** or gnocchi, ideally those made with butternut squash.

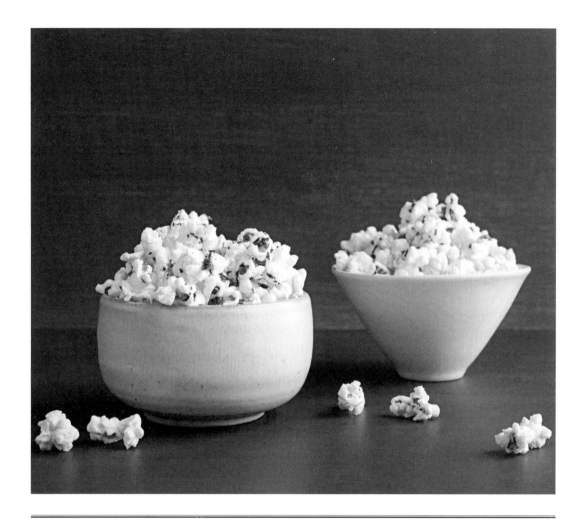

Hippie Popcorn

Place ¼ cup canola oil and ¼ cup popcorn kernels in a very large pot and cover with a lid. Have pot holders or kitchen towels ready. Heat over medium-high heat until you start to hear popping sounds, about 4 minutes.

Using pot holders, shake continuously over the heat. Continue to shake as the popping increases in speed. When it starts to slow down to a crawl (2 to 3 seconds between pops), after about 3 minutes,

take the pot off the heat and continue to shake until you no longer hear popping.

Immediately pour the popcorn into a large bowl. Drizzle with the herbed brown butter, sprinkle with 2 teaspoons nutritional yeast, and season to taste with salt. Toss well and serve immediately.
Makes about 12 cups

Fruity

The Mother Pomodoro . . . 70

Cherry Sherry Glaze . . . 72
[Sliced Duck Breast with Duck Fat Croutons]

Plum, Tangerine, and Five-Spice Jiang . . . 74
[Pan-Fried Pork Chops with Scallions]

Grape, Cilantro, Fresh Chile, and Lime Nam Chim . . . 76
[Rice Bowl with Marinated Grilled Chicken]

Pomegranate-Lemon Reduction . . . 78
[Fried Cauliflower with Pomegranate, Parsley, and Yogurt]

Cranapple Double-Ginger Relish . . . 80
[Homemade Granola and Yogurt Parfaits]

Fig and Balsamic Agrodolce . . . 82
[Pan-Roasted Pork Tenderloin with Rosemary]

Downright Upright Applesauce . . . 84
[Mashed Potato Pancakes with Sour Cream, Chives, and Bacon]

The Mother Pomodoro

Contrary to the popular misconception, the tomato is not a vegetable but a fruit. I consider tomato sauce a pantry staple—countless recipes call for it. Having an arsenal of sauce at the ready makes cooking dinner a snap, and the variations below allow you to keep your meals interesting with just a few additions. I usually make a big batch and keep some in my fridge for the week. The rest goes into plastic freezer-safe containers or zip-tight plastic bags for up to six months. Your grandmother may have spent all day cooking her famous sauce and I'm sure it was delicious, but if you don't have all day to spare, this quick iteration is pretty darn good, at a fraction of the labor time.

Makes about 3 cups

2 medium cloves garlic, chopped

¼ cup extra-virgin olive oil

1 (28-ounce) can crushed tomatoes

2 teaspoons dried Italian seasoning

1 tablespoon sugar

Sea salt

Pinch of crushed red pepper, optional

1. Combine the garlic and olive oil in a medium saucepan over medium-low heat. Cook, stirring occasionally, until the garlic just begins to soften and the oil is fragrant, about 4 minutes. Carefully stir in the tomatoes, dried herbs, and sugar. Raise the heat to medium, stir, and bring to a simmer. Continue to cook, stirring constantly, until the flavors develop and the sauce thickens slightly, about 20 minutes.

2. Stir in salt to taste. Add the crushed red pepper, if desired. Use immediately or store refrigerated in an airtight container for up to 1 week or freeze for up to 6 months.

Mix It Up

Customize the mother sauce to your taste, and to use in different ways.

Creamy Parmesan Pomodoro	**Puttanesca Sauce**	**Diavolo Sauce**	**Fresh Tomato, Herb, & Garlic Sauce**
Stir 6 tablespoons heavy cream, ½ cup finely grated Parmesan cheese, and ¼ cup packed chopped fresh basil over medium-low heat until smooth and creamy.	Mix in ¾ cup coarsely chopped pitted Kalamata olives, 2 teaspoons anchovy paste, and 1 tablespoon drained capers.	Add ½ cup chopped roasted red pepper, 1 chopped fresh Fresno or red jalapeño chile, and ¼ cup packed chopped fresh flat-leaf parsley and stir to combine.	Stir in 1½ cups chopped fresh tomatoes, ½ cup packed mixed chopped fresh herbs, such as oregano, parsley, rosemary, thyme, and basil, and 1 finely chopped garlic clove.

Extra Credit

- Any one of the tomato sauces will be a workhorse with any shaped **pasta**, on top of pizza, or as a dip for warm bread.

- Place some of the mother pomodoro in a few large butter-coated ramekins and top each with 1 to 2 **eggs** and a sprinkle of Parmesan. Bake at 400°F until the whites are opaque, 8 to 12 minutes.

- Roast potatoes, **broccoli**, eggplant, fennel, and green beans and serve with fresh tomato, herb, and garlic sauce for a bright and flavorful vegetarian feast.

- Use any one of these sauces to make a standout chicken or **eggplant Parm.**

CHERRY SHERRY GLAZE

This recipe is inspired by Ginjinha or Ginja, a tart cherry liqueur that's famous in Portugal. Ginja varies in quality from the cheap and artificial variety to the sublime, authentic, and (obviously) more expensive bottle. When I finally had some of the good stuff, I couldn't believe the flavor. Ginjinha is great to use in cooking, but since it can be difficult to locate, I used dry sherry and cherries as the base for this sauce instead. Cherry sherry glaze is a slightly sweet, tart, full-bodied sauce that is perfect for cutting through the richness of game meats, such as duck, venison, or goose, or with pork tenderloin or turkey. It's also fabulous as part of a cheese plate.

Makes about 2¼ cups

1 tablespoon extra-virgin olive oil

1 medium shallot, finely chopped

2 medium cloves garlic, finely chopped

2 cups pitted cherries, fresh or frozen and thawed

¾ cup dry sherry

1 bay leaf

¾ cup low-sodium chicken broth

2 tablespoons sugar

2 teaspoons cornstarch

2 tablespoons chopped fresh tarragon

2 tablespoons cold unsalted butter

Sea salt and freshly ground black pepper

1. Heat the olive oil in a large skillet over medium heat. Add the shallot and garlic and cook until fragrant, about 1 minute.

2. Turn the heat off and stir in the cherries, sherry, and bay leaf, then simmer over medium-high heat until the alcohol cooks off, about 8 minutes.

3. In a small bowl, whisk together the chicken broth, sugar, and cornstarch. Pour the chicken broth mixture into the cherry mixture, bring to a boil, and cook, stirring occasionally, until slightly thickened, 3 to 4 minutes. Turn the heat off and whisk in the tarragon and butter until the sauce is slightly thickened and glossy. Season to taste with salt and pepper. The sauce will keep in the refrigerator for several days.

Extra Credit

• Serve in place of cranberry sauce to accompany **turkey or chicken at Thanksgiving** or whenever.

• Drizzle over **sautéed kale** or baby bok choy for a sweet and savory combo.

• Mix some of the cooled cherry sherry glaze with softened butter and use as a topping for biscuits or **scones**.

• Sandwich some **roasted pork** between two pieces of multigrain or rye bread along with bitter greens, such as arugula or dandelion, some Dijon mustard, and cherry sherry glaze.

Sliced Duck Breast with Duck Fat Croutons

Preheat the oven to 375°F. Ready a parchment-lined baking sheet. Place 4 duck breasts, about 6 ounces each, skin side up on a cutting board and pat dry. Using a sharp knife, make 4 or 5 parallel slits on a diagonal, cutting just through the skin. Rotate the breasts 45 degrees and score in the other direction, creating a diamond pattern. Sprinkle all over with salt and pepper.

Heat a large cast-iron or ovenproof heavy-bottomed skillet over medium-high heat. When the pan is hot, add the duck breasts, skin side down, to the pan. Cook until the fat is rendered and the skin is golden brown and crisp, about 5 minutes. Use tongs to flip the duck breasts over and sear for 4 minutes more. Transfer to the prepared baking sheet.

Pour the duck fat into a small bowl and reserve the skillet. Cut 3 cups worth of rustic bread into 2-inch cubes. Scatter the bread cubes around the duck breasts on the baking sheet and drizzle with 3 tablespoons of the reserved duck fat. Lightly season the bread cubes with salt. Transfer the pan to the oven and roast until the duck is cooked through, 10 to 12 minutes. Let the duck rest for about 5 minutes.

Transfer the duck breasts to a cutting board and slice each across the grain. Place each breast on a plate along with some of the croutons. Drizzle with warm cherry sherry glaze and serve immediately.
Serves 4

PLUM, TANGERINE, AND FIVE-SPICE JIANG

It's hard to find a perfectly ripe plum in the supermarket. They usually seem dry, too tart, and obviously picked before their prime. That's too bad because fresh, perfectly ripe plums are incredibly juicy, sweet, and fragrant with a delicate slightly floral flavor. So I have devised ways of sugaring, cooking, baking, and otherwise preserving them to try to keep that flavor going as long as I can. This recipe was inspired by my need to make underripe plums taste good and also by the moo shu from our local Chinese restaurant. To me, the one element that makes moo shu worth the price of admission is the smear of rich, sweet, thick plum sauce or jiang. My version is chunky and a lot fresher tasting than the standard variety. Try it served with Chinese fare but also any rich meat, from pork and dark meat turkey to duck or goose.

Makes about 3 cups

¼ cup fresh tangerine juice, squeezed from 2 tangerines

1 teaspoon cornstarch

1 tablespoon canola oil

1 tablespoon grated fresh ginger

2 medium cloves garlic, thinly sliced

1½ pounds ripe plums (about 5), halved, pitted, and coarsely chopped

2 tablespoons finely chopped fresh tangerine peel

⅓ cup dark brown sugar

1 teaspoon five-spice powder

2 tablespoons low-sodium soy sauce

Sea salt

1. In a small bowl, whisk the tangerine juice with the cornstarch until the cornstarch dissolves.

2. Heat the oil over medium heat in a large skillet. Add the ginger and garlic and cook until fragrant, about 1 minute.

3. Add the plums, tangerine peel, brown sugar, five-spice powder, and ¼ cup water and stir to combine. Cook, stirring, until the plums are heated through but still hold their shape, about 8 minutes.

4. Stir in the tangerine juice mixture, bring to a simmer, and cook until slightly thickened, about 3 minutes. Stir in the soy sauce and season to taste with salt. Serve immediately or store refrigerated in an airtight container for up to 3 days.

Extra Credit

- Bathe **pulled pork** in this jiang instead of regular barbecue sauce, then make sandwiches with soft buns and shredded cabbage.

- Make an easy **lunch bowl** by tossing brown rice, lettuce, chopped scallions, cilantro, and cooked shredded chicken with the sauce.

- Serve this sauce in place of cranberry sauce alongside dark meat chicken or **turkey** to throw some Chinese flair into Thanksgiving.

- Skip ordering takeout and toss wide rice **noodles** and sautéed kale with the sauce instead.

Pan-Fried Pork Chops with Scallions

Bring four ¾-inch-thick, center-cut, bone-in pork chops (about 2 pounds total) to room temperature. Pat dry using paper towels and liberally season all over with salt and pepper.

Heat a large cast-iron or heavy-bottomed skillet over medium-high heat and, once hot, add about 1 tablespoon canola oil. Add the pork chops and let cook without moving until they are golden brown on one side, 3 to 4 minutes. Flip and cook the remaining side until golden brown and cooked through, 3 to 4 minutes more. Transfer to a platter and let rest about 5 minutes.

Add 8 whole scallions to the pan used for the pork chops. Over medium heat, sear them slightly (about 3 to 4 minutes). Serve each chop with a couple scallions and the plum sauce on top, with rice on the side if you like. **Serves 4**

Maceration, when applied in the culinary sense, is a term most often reserved for fruit: You add liquor, vinegar, and/or sugar to draw the moisture out, soften up the flesh, and add flavor, creating a sauce-like syrup.

GRAPE, CILANTRO, FRESH CHILE, AND LIME NAM CHIM

I love fresh grapes, but I always find it hard to get through a whole bag. Here's a great way to use the stray leftovers before they become squishy. Sweet, savory, tart, and a little spicy all in one, this Thai-inspired fresh sauce will expand your grape repertoire, or should I say your grape-toire. It's sure to enhance anything lean and grilled. I suggest a mix of different colors of grapes here, but if you have just one variety on hand, it will still come out just as tasty.

Makes about 1¾ cups

½ cup green seedless grapes, coarsely chopped

½ cup red seedless grapes, coarsely chopped

½ cup black seedless grapes, coarsely chopped

Half of 1 medium jalapeño, seeded and finely chopped

1 teaspoon lime zest

1 tablespoon fresh lime juice

1 tablespoon fish sauce

½ cup packed roughly chopped fresh cilantro

In a medium bowl, combine the grapes, jalapeño, lime zest, lime juice, fish sauce, and cilantro. Stir to combine and let sit at room temperature for about 30 minutes, tossing once or twice until the flavors develop. Use immediately or store refrigerated in an airtight container for up to 2 days.

Extra Credit

• Spoon some of the sauce over cooked chicken and more cilantro in a flour tortilla for an Asian–Mexican **fusion wrap**.

• Stir ½ cup canola oil into the sauce, then toss with shredded green and red cabbage for a tangy **Asian-style slaw**.

• Toss the nam chim sauce with leftover **wild rice** and fresh torn basil for a quick side dish.

• Pulse the sauce in a food processor until finely chopped, stir in a few splashes of rice vinegar, and serve with raw **oysters** on the half shell for a Thai-style mignonette.

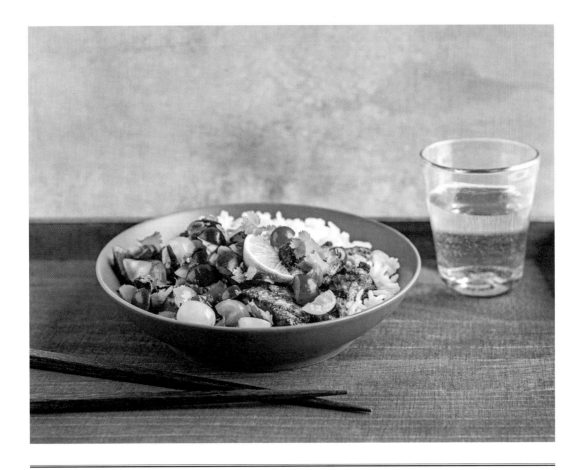

Rice Bowl with Marinated Grilled Chicken

In a large bowl, whisk together 1 tablespoon canola oil, 2 tablespoons low-sodium soy sauce, 1 tablespoon fish sauce, 2 tablespoons dark brown sugar, 2 tablespoons fresh lime juice, 2 teaspoons lime zest, 1 teaspoon grated fresh ginger, 1 teaspoon garlic powder, and 1 tablespoon curry powder.

Add 2 boneless, skinless chicken breasts (1¼ pounds total) sliced into 1-inch cubes directly into the bowl and toss thoroughly to coat with the marinade. Cover and refrigerate for about 1 hour. Meanwhile, soak four 10-inch wooden skewers in water for about 30 minutes before using them.

Evenly divide and thread the chicken breasts onto the skewers. Discard any leftover marinade. Preheat a grill or grill pan to medium-high heat. Lightly oil the grill and cook the chicken pieces on all sides until grill marks form and the chicken is cooked through, about 10 minutes total.

Carefully slide the grilled chicken off the skewers into four bowls filled with cooked rice. Top each with some of the nam chim sauce and garnish with crushed roasted peanuts, a lime wedge, and cilantro sprigs. **Serves 4**

POMEGRANATE-LEMON REDUCTION

Pomegranate molasses is one of the quintessential Middle Eastern sauces. It adds an acidic burst that cuts right through fatty meats like beef or lamb, fried foods, creamy desserts—anything rich, really—and its deep ruby color is beautiful to behold. I used to buy it in specialty food shops, but after moving away from Brooklyn, I've found it tricky to locate. Now I make my own. As you'll see it's easy as ABC. Just remember, it turns quickly from syrup to burnt candy, so don't get any ideas about going on a beer run while it's on the stove. My version is more lemony and less sweet than the store-bought type. One of the perks of being your own saucier is the ability to tweak recipes according to your own taste.

Make about ½ cup

2 cups pomegranate juice

2 tablespoons sugar

1 teaspoon lemon zest

1 tablespoon fresh lemon juice

1. Combine the pomegranate juice, sugar, and lemon zest in a medium saucepan and bring to a boil over high heat, stirring occasionally until the sugar dissolves, about 4 minutes.

2. Continue to boil, stirring occasionally, until thickened slightly and reduced to ½ cup, about 12 minutes. Stir in the lemon juice. Cool to room temperature and then store refrigerated in a squirt bottle or an airtight container for up to 1 month.

Extra Credit

● Mix the pomegranate-lemon reduction with seltzer water, an extra splash of fresh lemon juice, crushed fresh mint leaves, and ice cubes for a nifty **spritzer**. Add vodka to up the ante.

● Drizzle the sauce over **ice cream** and top with chopped pistachios.

● Use as a dip for spiced chicken or **beef kebabs**.

● Spoon onto fruit salad to add a red flavor jolt. Or stir into vanilla, lemon, or plain **yogurt** for a healthy snack.

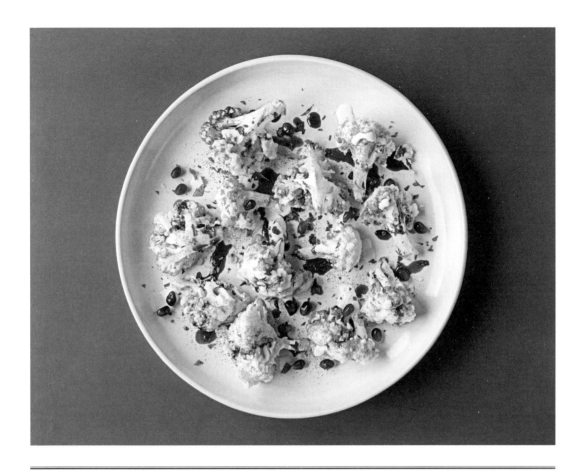

Fried Cauliflower with Pomegranate, Parsley, and Yogurt

Cut one head of cauliflower into 2-inch florets and set aside. You should have about 6 cups florets. Combine 2 large eggs, ½ cup room temperature water, and 1 teaspoon salt in a bowl and whisk until frothy. Add ¾ cup cornstarch and whisk until a smooth thin batter is formed.

Pour 1 inch canola oil (about 6 cups) into a large pot and heat over medium-high heat until a drop of the batter sizzles in the oil. Dip a few cauliflower florets at a time into the batter, and then gently drop them into the hot oil. Fry in batches, flipping once during cooking until golden brown and crisp,

4 to 5 minutes per batch. If the oil starts smoking during the process, turn down the heat. Transfer to a paper towel–lined plate to drain and sprinkle lightly with salt, then transfer to a platter.

In a small bowl, whisk together 3 tablespoons plain whole-milk yogurt and 1 tablespoon water. Drizzle the cauliflower with the yogurt and some of the pomegranate-lemon reduction. Sprinkle with ¼ teaspoon ground cumin, 3 tablespoons fresh pomegranate seeds, and 1 to 2 tablespoons fresh chopped flat-leaf parsley. Serve immediately. **Serves 4**

CRANAPPLE DOUBLE-GINGER RELISH

Yes, you can eat cranberries raw. When I was a kid, I used to dip them in sugar and pop them directly in my mouth. Admittedly, I was a bit of a strange child. But I stand by the idea: the crisp and airy texture of the berry mixed with sugar works—try it. I also add the raw berries to smoothies in the blender. For me, cooking cranberries has its place (compotes, pie filling, etc.), but using them raw shouldn't be overlooked. It allows them to retain their bite and inherent freshness. In general, I consider cranberries underrated—it's a shame people forget about them after Thanksgiving. Since cranberries are seasonal, I recommend buying the fresh berries in bulk and freezing them; they will last the year.

This sauce takes advantage of the zing of the fresh berries and fresh ginger. Mixed with the crisp sweet apple and mild sweetness of the brown rice syrup, it's a match made in heaven. You can make it with or without the nuts, but if you're a nut fiend like myself, the more the better.

Make about 2 cups

½ cup raw pecans

1½ cups fresh cranberries

2 fresh apples such as Honey Crisp or Gala, peeled, cored, and coarsely chopped (about 2 cups)

½ teaspoon grated fresh ginger

3 tablespoons brown rice syrup

2 tablespoons finely chopped crystallized ginger

1. Preheat the oven to 400°F. Scatter the pecans on a baking sheet and place in the oven, tossing once halfway through cooking, until golden brown inside and toasted on the outside, 8 to 10 minutes. Let cool slightly, then coarsely chop.

2. Combine the cranberries, apples, grated ginger, and brown rice syrup in a food processor and pulse about 40 times until finely chopped. Transfer to a medium bowl. Stir in the crystallized ginger and pecans until well combined. Serve immediately or store refrigerated in an airtight container for up to 1 week.

Extra Credit

● Spoon this relish on top of pancakes, waffles, or **French toast** for a zippy alternative to maple syrup.

● Serve as a condiment alongside a **turkey and stuffing** dinner in place of cooked cranberry relish or sauce.

● Top a slice of store-bought **pound cake** with the sauce and a dollop of sweetened whipped cream.

● For an insta-snack, top a piece of toasted **rustic bread** or crackers with butter and the relish.

Homemade Granola and Yogurt Parfaits

To make the granola, preheat the oven to 325°F. In a large bowl, combine 2 cups old-fashioned rolled oats, ¼ cup millet, ½ cup coarsely chopped raw almonds, and ½ cup raw, hulled pumpkin seeds. In a medium bowl, stir together ¼ cup canola oil, 2 tablespoons raw sesame seeds, ½ cup brown rice syrup, and ½ teaspoon salt. Pour the syrup mixture over the oat mixture and mix thoroughly to combine. (This makes more than you'll need—about 7 cups granola. Store it in an airtight container for up to 3 weeks; it makes a great gift.)

Spread the oat mixture out onto a parchment-lined baking sheet and bake, tossing a few times during the cooking process, until the granola is golden and crisp, 40 to 45 minutes. Transfer the pan to a wire rack to cool completely.

Break up the granola into smaller chunks over a large bowl and stir in ½ cup dried cherries, ½ cup golden raisins, and ½ cup pitted chopped Medjool dates.

To assemble the parfaits, spoon ¼ cup plain whole-milk yogurt into the bottom of each of four parfait glasses and top with ¼ cup cranapple relish and a few tablespoons of the granola. Repeat the process twice, ending with the granola. Garnish each parfait with a fresh sprig of mint, if desired.
Serves 4

FIG AND BALSAMIC AGRODOLCE

Fond of figs? You're in luck because this recipe is based on fond and figs. Fond is culinary snob speak for the brown bits left over after you roast meat and vegetables. When scraped from the bottom of the pan, the fond (which in French literally means "bottom") can be incorporated into a sauce, adding a ton of rich depth and caramelized goodness. To achieve the sublimity of this sauce, there is a prerequisite: it's based on your having already roasted some meat and/or vegetables in a skillet. This could be beef, chicken, and/or root vegetables—anything that can get nice and browned in the oven or on the stovetop. See the pork tenderloin recipe below for one suggestion.

Makes about 2 cups

1 large heavy-bottomed skillet with fond (see above)

2 tablespoons unsalted butter plus 2 tablespoons cold unsalted butter, cut into small pieces

¼ cup thinly sliced shallots

1 cup coarsely chopped dried figs, such as Mission or Turkish

1 tablespoon chopped fresh rosemary

½ cup balsamic vinegar

1 cup reduced-sodium chicken or beef broth

1. Drain any excess fat from the skillet. Melt 2 tablespoons of the butter in the skillet over medium heat. Add the shallots, and cook, stirring occasionally and scraping up any brown bits from the pan.

2. Continue to cook until the shallots begin to soften, about 3 minutes. Add the figs and rosemary and stir to combine. Add the balsamic, bring to a simmer, and cook until the vinegar starts to thicken slightly, about 4 minutes. Add the broth and simmer until reduced slightly, about 10 minutes.

3. Turn off the heat and slowly whisk in the 2 tablespoons cold butter. Serve immediately.

Extra Credit

• Serve fig and balsamic agrodolce with pan-seared chicken or **lamb chops** instead of pork.

• Use as part of a **cheese plate**: my go-to cheeses to pair with this sauce are Parmesan, Gorgonzola dolce, Robiola, and pecorino. Don't forget to serve nuts as well.

• Top a roasted **sweet potato** with some leftover sauce and a dollop of mascarpone.

• Cook some sliced sausage, reserving the fond in the skillet to make the sauce. Spread the sauce on **pizza** dough, sprinkle with the sausage, and bake. Scatter with fresh arugula.

Pan-Roasted Pork Tenderloin with Rosemary

Preheat the oven to 400°F. Heat a large cast-iron or ovenproof heavy-bottomed skillet over medium-high heat. Season a room-temperature 1¼-pound pork tenderloin all over with salt and pepper. When the skillet is very hot, add 1 tablespoon olive oil and the pork and sear on all sides, about 6 minutes total.

Roast the pork in the skillet until a meat thermometer inserted into the center registers 140°F. Transfer the pork to a cutting board to rest,

covered loosely with foil, for about 10 minutes. Reserve the skillet.

Slice the pork against the grain, drizzle with the fig and balsamic agrodolce sauce, and garnish with more fresh rosemary leaves. Serve immediately or store the sauce refrigerated in an airtight container for up to 3 days. Bring to room temperature or rewarm slightly before using, taking care not to break the butter. **Serves 4**

DOWNRIGHT UPRIGHT APPLESAUCE

When our daughter was just beginning to eat solid foods, I occasionally made my own baby food for her. One time, after making a much too large batch of applesauce, I decided to spiff it up with some Calvados (apple brandy) and served it with cake and cream. Thus was born my spiked applesauce. The alcohol is boiled off so you can feed this to youngsters if you wish (that's why I call it "upright"). But the slightly floral fragrance of apples remains from the Calvados. I use a variety of apples to get a sweet and tart flavor combination. The versatile result is great eaten alone with a spoon, used as a yogurt topping, or as a condiment for roast pork tenderloin.

Makes about 3½ cups

½ cup apple cider

¼ cup apple cider vinegar

2 tablespoons dark brown sugar

¼ cup Calvados or other apple brandy

1 pound (2 to 3) Honeycrisp or Gala apples, peeled, cored, and roughly chopped

1 pound Golden Delicious apples, peeled, cored, and roughly chopped

½ pound (1 to 2) Granny Smith apples, peeled, cored, and roughly chopped

1. In a medium saucepan, combine the apple cider, vinegar, brown sugar, and brandy and bring to a boil over medium-high heat, about 4 minutes.

2. Stir in the apples, cover the pot, and reduce the heat to medium-low. Cook until the apples are very soft, 20 to 25 minutes.

3. Use a potato masher to smash the mixture for a chunkier applesauce; for a smooth texture, use an immersion blender or transfer to a food processor and process until puréed. Let cool to room temperature, then transfer to the refrigerator to cool completely. Store refrigerated in an airtight container for up to 1 week.

- Serve as a sweet condiment alongside pan-fried **pork chops** and fried onions.

- Make a **smoothie** with some sauce, a banana, whole milk, raw almonds, flax seeds, and a handful of ice cubes.

- Flavor your applesauce by blending it with fresh strawberries or peaches, cinnamon, nutmeg, and a bit of vanilla. Use as an **oatmeal topper**.

- Give your own spin to storebought frozen potato **pierogies** by serving with this sauce and some snipped chives for a party.

Mashed Potato Pancakes with Sour Cream, Chives, and Bacon

Peel 2½ pounds russet potatoes (about 3 large potatoes) and cut into ½-inch pieces. Place in a large pot and add enough cold water to cover by 2 inches. Bring to a boil over high heat and boil until the potatoes are tender, about 20 minutes total. Drain the potatoes, then press them through a ricer or smash them with a potato masher into a large bowl. You should have 5 cups mashed potatoes.

Let cool slightly, for about 10 minutes, then add ½ cup all-purpose flour, 2 large eggs, 2 teaspoons salt, and ½ teaspoon black pepper and stir to thoroughly combine. Form the potato mixture into 8 equal-sized balls, then press each ball into a 4- by 1-inch pancake and place on a parchment-lined baking sheet. Arrange three large shallow dishes or plates side by side. Fill one with 1 cup all-purpose flour, one with 2 beaten large eggs, and one with 3 cups panko breadcrumbs. Dip each pancake in the flour, then the eggs, then the breadcrumbs. Place each cake back on the prepared baking sheet and refrigerate until firm, 30 minutes to 1 hour.

Meanwhile, cut 4 slices thick-cut bacon into ½-inch pieces. Cook the bacon in a large high-sided skillet, stirring occasionally, until crisp, about 5 minutes. Transfer the bacon to a paper towel–lined plate to drain, reserving the fat in the skillet.

When the pancakes are chilled, reheat the skillet over medium heat. Add 1 tablespoon canola oil and a few pancakes and cook for 6 to 8 minutes total, flipping them over halfway through cooking, until dark golden and crisp on both sides. Repeat with the remaining pancakes, adding more oil as needed. Transfer to a paper towel–lined plate to drain. Transfer to plates and top with dollops of sour cream, a large spoonful of downright upright applesauce, fresh chopped chives, and the crumbled bacon. Serve immediately. **Serves 4**

Nutty

The Mother Tahini . . . 88

Not as Slowly Mole . . . 90
[Baked Cheese Enchiladas]

Walnut and Sage Bagna Cauda . . . 92
[Roasted Whole Carrots with Labneh]

Thai Satay . . . 94
[Fresh Summer Rolls]

Poppy Seed and Parmesan Gloss . . . 98
[Orecchiette with Rainbow Chard and Bread Crumbs]

Golden Romesco . . . 100
[Marinated Grilled Calamari Kebabs]

Butternut Curry Cashew Cream . . . 102
[Tofu and Root Vegetable Stew]

Pistachio Crème . . . 104
[Crispy Salmon with Pea Greens]

The Mother Tahini

A staple of Middle Eastern cuisine, tahini is essentially sesame seeds ground into a paste. By itself it has a consistency similar to peanut butter. When you purchase it, you generally have to mix the oil and seed butter together, as they tend to separate in the jar. The flavor differs among brands; some might be slightly more bitter than others. I tend to like tahini on the milder side. To turn it into a sauce, you simply need to mix in some liquid and seasonings. It's just what you need atop a falafel or shawarma pita sandwich, but experiment a little and you will soon find a million other ways to use it.

Makes about ¾ cup

½ cup tahini

2 tablespoons fresh lemon juice

Sea salt

Whisk together the tahini, ⅓ cup hot water, and the lemon juice in a medium bowl. Season to taste with salt. Use immediately or store in an airtight container in the refrigerator for up to 1 week (whisk again before using if oil from the sauce separates).

Mix It Up

Customize the mother sauce to your taste, and to use in different ways.

Parsley, Carrot, & Cumin Tahini

Stir in ½ cup finely grated fresh carrot, ¼ cup chopped fresh flat-leaf parsley, and 1 teaspoon ground cumin.

Roasted Garlic, Coriander, & Yogurt Tahini

Whisk in 8 chopped cloves roasted garlic, ½ teaspoon ground coriander, and ¼ cup Greek yogurt or labneh.

Sesame Oil, Scallion, & Soy Sauce Tahini

Stir in 1 teaspoon toasted sesame oil, ⅓ cup thinly sliced scallions, and 4 teaspoons low-sodium soy sauce.

Honey, Vanilla, & Black Pepper Tahini

Whisk in the seeds of 1 scraped vanilla bean, 3 tablespoons honey, and a pinch of freshly ground black pepper.

Extra Credit

- Stir the honey, vanilla, and black pepper tahini into yogurt and top with chopped nuts, dates, and fresh fruit for an instant and **healthy breakfast**. Try it also drizzled on crisp apple slices.

- For at-home Chinese takeout, toss the sesame oil, scallion, and soy sauce tahini with warm or cold **soba noodles**. Garnish with more scallions and toasted sesame seeds.

- Serve the carrot, roasted garlic, or mother tahini sauce with any grilled meat or chicken, especially in **kebab** form.

- For an easy side-dish salad, toss the carrot, garlic, or mother tahini sauce with chickpeas, chopped parsley, chopped red bell pepper, and **Israeli couscous**.

NOT AS SLOWLY MOLE

The Aztec word *mole* simply translates as "mix." This helps explain why the term is something of a catchall for a large range of sauces. One thing that is almost always constant, though, is the inclusion of some sort of ground-up nut or seed. Making classic rich brown moles is typically a long and laborious process. Often they call for more than a dozen ingredients, many of which must be individually toasted, charred, sautéed, crushed, and/or chopped by hand. This sweet and salty mole still has a long ingredient list, but it takes a fraction of the time of a traditional version. I usually eat it with roast chicken or turkey, but it also makes a lovely taco topping, burrito addition, or sauce for enchiladas as in the recipe at right.

Makes about 2 cups

1 tablespoon canola oil

2 tablespoons slivered raw almonds

½ cup chopped white onion

1 dried chile pepper, such as ancho or mulato, seeds and stem removed, torn or cut into small pieces

⅓ cup stale bread torn into small pieces

1 tablespoon raw sesame seeds

¼ cup raisins

2 medium cloves garlic, chopped

2 tablespoons raw hulled pumpkin seeds

1½ cups low-sodium chicken broth

2 tablespoons roasted unsalted peanuts

¼ teaspoon ground cinnamon

½ teaspoon ground cumin

½ teaspoon ground coriander

6 tablespoons finely chopped dark chocolate

Sea salt

1. Heat the oil in a medium saucepan over medium-high heat. Add the almonds and cook until just beginning to toast, about 4 minutes. Add the onions and cook, stirring occasionally, until soft, about 4 minutes.

2. Add the chile pepper, bread, and sesame seeds and cook, stirring occasionally, until the seeds are lightly toasted, about 6 minutes. Add the raisins, garlic, and pumpkin seeds and cook until fragrant, about 1 minute.

3. Pour in the chicken broth and bring the mixture to a boil over high heat. Cook until the chile softens, about 5 minutes.

4. Pour the broth mixture into a high-powered blender along with the peanuts, cinnamon, cumin, coriander, and chocolate and blend until smooth. Season to taste with salt. Serve immediately or store refrigerated in an airtight container for up to 2 weeks.

Extra Credit

- Add cooked shredded chicken, **fresh corn**, or chopped green chiles, or all three to the enchiladas.

- Make **quesadillas** filled with thinly sliced mango and jack cheese, sprinkled with queso blanco over the top, and served with the mole for dipping.

- Grill some **steaks** along with whole scallions and fresh corn tortillas, serve with the mole, and you have a serious party.

- Pan-roast a couple **duck breast** halves, drape with the sauce, sprinkle toasted sesame seeds over the top, and serve with wild rice.

Baked Cheese Enchiladas

Preheat the oven to 400°F. Wrap twelve 5-inch-diameter corn tortillas in foil and warm them in the oven until pliable, about 15 minutes.

Meanwhile, grate 2½ cups (about 10 ounces) Jack cheese and set aside. Pour 1 cup of the mole into the bottom of an 8- by 8-inch baking dish. Remove one tortilla at a time from the foil and top each with 2 tablespoons shredded cheese. Fold the tortilla in half and place in the baking dish. Repeat with the remaining tortillas and most of the cheese to form two overlapping rows.

Drizzle the tortillas with the remaining 1 cup mole and sprinkle with the remaining cheese. Cover the baking dish with foil, return to the oven, and bake until the cheese has melted, about 15 minutes. Serve the enchiladas garnished with chopped white onion, cilantro, and fresh chopped avocado. **Serves 4**

The word *chocolate* comes from the Aztec *xocolatl*, which translates as "bitter water." Mexicans have used unsweetened chocolate in savory dishes for centuries (mole being the classic case). But Italians also took to the idea and use it in some pasta sauces.

WALNUT AND SAGE BAGNA CAUDA

Bagna cauda is a classic Italian sauce traditionally served warm and in the style of fondue with lots of veggies and bread to use as dipping agents. While the purist's version is made with garlic, olive oil, and anchovies, my take, admittedly a very loose reinterpretation, uses browned butter, sage, and walnuts. Serve it as a dip for veggies and crusty bread as you would the original. Or spoon this rich concoction over meat, fish, or pasta. Buon appetito!

Makes about ½ cup

½ cup raw walnut halves

6 tablespoons unsalted butter

2 medium cloves garlic, chopped

2 tablespoons chopped fresh sage leaves

2 teaspoons fresh lemon juice

Sea salt

1. Preheat the oven to 400°F. Scatter the walnuts on a baking sheet and place in the oven, tossing once halfway through, until golden brown inside and toasted on the outside, 8 to 10 minutes. Transfer to a food processor and pulse until finely ground.

2. Melt the butter in a medium saucepan over medium heat. When the butter has melted, add the garlic and cook, stirring occasionally, until the garlic is fragrant and the butter takes on a nutty aroma, about 4 minutes. Stir in the sage leaves and turn off the heat. Stir in the ground walnuts and the lemon juice. Season to taste with salt. Serve warm.

Extra Credit

- Toss with **pasta** and some fresh arugula and grated Parmesan cheese.

- Roast split **acorn squash**, fill the cavities with barley or farro, and drizzle the sauce over all.

- Toss the sauce with cubed toasted bread, then toss with a beaten egg and just enough milk and/or stock to moisten; bake until crusty for a divine **bread stuffing**.

- Stir into plain cooked oats for a **savory porridge** on a cold night.

Roasted Whole Carrots with Labneh

Preheat the oven to 425°F. Cut off the leafy greens from 16 small to medium carrots and reserve for another use (such as in the carrot-top, kale, and lemon pesto on page 51). Scrub any dirt off of the carrots. Place on a parchment-lined baking sheet and toss with 1 tablespoon olive oil, ½ teaspoon sea salt, and ½ teaspoon freshly ground black pepper. Roast the carrots, tossing once or twice, until golden in parts, about 30 minutes.

Remove from the oven and drizzle 1 tablespoon honey over the carrots. Return to the oven and continue to roast until golden brown and caramelized, about 5 minutes more.

Transfer to a serving plate. Drizzle with the bagna cauda, dollop with labneh (Middle Eastern strained yogurt), and top with a handful of fresh parsley leaves. Serve warm. **Serves 4**

THAI SATAY

When we order Thai food, we ask for extra peanut sauce but never seem to get as much as we want. So, when you can't beat them, join them: I started making my own. It is quite simple if you have the ingredients on hand, and luckily, most are pantry staples. A mixture of sweet, salty, creamy, slightly tart, and spicy, this sauce lends itself to more flavorful cold crispy vegetables, hot grilled meats, and noodles.

Makes about 2 cups

1 tablespoon canola oil

1 tablespoon finely chopped fresh ginger

1 medium shallot, finely chopped

1 medium clove garlic, finely chopped

1 cup natural smooth peanut butter

1 tablespoon lime zest

¼ cup fresh lime juice

¼ cup packed dark brown sugar

¼ teaspoon crushed red pepper

2 tablespoons fish sauce

1. Heat the oil in a medium saucepan over medium-low heat. Add the ginger, shallot, and garlic and cook, stirring occasionally, until softened, about 4 minutes.

2. Add ¾ cup water and bring to a simmer, about 2 minutes. Turn the heat off and stir in the peanut butter, lime juice, lime zest, brown sugar, crushed red pepper, and fish sauce until smooth. Serve at room temperature or store refrigerated in an airtight container for up to 1 week. Thin out with a couple tablespoons hot water if necessary.

Use your imagination when it comes to the filling components of summer rolls. Think of this recipe as just a blueprint. For instance, you could swap cooked shredded chicken breast for the shrimp, cooked sweet potato for the avocado, or cucumber for the cabbage.

Extra Credit

- For a splendid yet simple cold noodle salad, toss the peanut sauce with cooked and cooled **soba noodles**, chopped scallions, shelled edamame, and sesame seeds.

- Thin out the sauce with a few tablespoons of water and rice vinegar to turn into a peanutty **salad dressing**. Toss some with cucumbers, shredded Napa cabbage, carrots, and sliced raw snow peas.

- Roast spears of skin-on **sweet potato** until browned, then serve with the sauce for dipping.

- Thin with coconut milk, then simmer chicken thighs and cut-up potatoes in the sauce for an extra-rich **curry**.

Fresh Summer Rolls

Cook 3 ounces dried thin rice or mung bean vermicelli according to the package directions. Run under cold water and drain.

Place 16 cooked, peeled, and deveined medium-size shrimp on a cutting board. Use a knife to slice each shrimp in half horizontally. Place ½ cup fresh mint leaves; 1 cup fresh cilantro sprigs; 1 cup basil leaves; 1 pitted, peeled, and thinly sliced avocado; 1 peeled, pitted, and thinly sliced mango; and 2 cups shredded purple cabbage in separate piles or containers around your work surface. Fill a large shallow dish with very hot water. Ready 8 round rice wrappers, 10 inches in diameter.

Working quickly with one wrapper at a time, completely submerge the wrapper in the water until it is soft and pliable, 10 to 15 seconds.

Remove the wrapper from the water and place on a cutting board. Lay 4 shrimp halves in a row, cut side up, in the center of the wrapper, leaving about an inch of space on both sides. Top with a few slices of avocado, a few mint leaves, a couple sprigs of cilantro and basil leaves, a few slices of mango, ¼ cup cabbage, and ¼ cup noodles. Fold the bottom half of the rice paper wrapper over the filling, then fold in the sides of the wrapper. Pressing down firmly, hold the folds in place and then tightly roll the wrapper up from bottom to top. Turn the roll over, seam side down, so that the shrimp faces up, and transfer to a large plate.

Repeat the process with the remaining 7 wrappers and filling ingredients and cover the plate with plastic wrap until ready to serve. Serve at room temperature with a side of Thai satay for dipping.

POPPY SEED AND PARMESAN GLOSS

I love the light crunch and earthy flavor that poppy seeds bring to dishes. Occasionally someone in my cooking classes asks if poppy seeds are narcotic, knowing that opiates are derived from poppies. In a word, no. Opium is found in the pod of the poppy and not in the seed itself. So you can rest assured that any strange behavior among your dinner guests cannot be blamed on this recipe. It will however offer plenty of less psycho-active delights. This is really the only sauce in the book that is based on a roux, a classic sauce-making technique.

Makes about 1 cup

3 tablespoons unsalted butter

2 medium garlic cloves, finely chopped

¼ cup dry white wine

2 tablespoons all-purpose flour

⅔ cup low-sodium chicken broth or vegetable broth

1 tablespoon poppy seeds

⅓ cup freshly grated Parmesan

1 teaspoon fresh lemon juice

Sea salt and freshly ground black pepper

1. In a medium cast-iron or heavy-bottomed skillet, melt the butter over medium-low heat. Add the garlic and cook, stirring, until fragrant and softened, about 2 minutes. Pour in the wine, bring to a simmer, and cook until reduced by about half, about 4 minutes. Whisk in the flour all at once and continue to cook and whisk for 2 to 3 minutes. Whisk in the broth and increase the heat to medium-high. Bring to a simmer, continuing to whisk until the sauce thickens.

2. Turn off the heat and stir in the poppy seeds, cheese, and lemon juice. Season to taste with salt and pepper. Use immediately or store refrigerated in an airtight container for up to 1 week. To rewarm, place the gloss in a bowl over a pot of simmering water. Stir occasionally until warmed through.

Extra Credit

• Dress up plain **cooked beets** (or any root vegetable like young top-on carrots or steamed green beans) with this glossy sauce; it'll make them worthy of a dinner party.

• Stir into **sautéed onions**, and use as a topping for a bagel or toast for a snack.

• For an easy, hearty meal, add chopped toasted walnuts and fresh chopped parsley to the sauce and then toss with shredded rotisserie chicken and **kasha** (buckwheat groats) or boiled potatoes.

• Take frozen store-bought **pierogies** to a whole new level by coating them with this sauce.

Orecchiette with Rainbow Chard and Bread Crumbs

Put a large pot of salted water onto medium-high heat to boil. Wash and dry 1¼ pounds rainbow chard. Coarsely chop both leaves and stems separately. You should wind up with about 8 cups chopped leaves and 2 cups chopped stems.

Cook 1 pound orecchiette in the boiling water until al dente according to package directions. Meanwhile, warm 2 tablespoons olive oil in a large high-sided skillet over medium heat. Add 2 cups freshly torn bread crumbs and a pinch of salt and cook, stirring occasionally until golden, crisp, and lightly toasted. Transfer to a small bowl.

Use a paper towel to wipe out the skillet and heat 3 tablespoons olive oil and 4 lightly smashed garlic cloves over medium heat until the oil is fragrant and the garlic is golden brown, 2 to 3 minutes. Remove the garlic with a slotted spoon.

Raise the heat to medium-high and add the chopped chard stems. Season lightly and cook, stirring occasionally, until crisp tender and caramelized, about 5 minutes. Add the chopped chard leaves, 1 tablespoon lemon zest, and a pinch of crushed red pepper and toss until the leaves are wilted, 2 to 3 minutes.

Drain the pasta in a colander. Add the pasta and the poppy seed sauce to the skillet and toss to combine with the chard. Season to taste. **Serves 4**

GOLDEN ROMESCO

A rustic Catalonian sauce originally intended to go with seafood, romesco is a harmonious mélange of tomatoes, peppers, nuts, garlic, and vinegar. The nuts, along with stale bread, not only add flavor, but thicken the sauce. It is generally red, but I love the sweetness that comes along with yellow tomatoes and yellow peppers; my romesco is not rust-colored but golden.

Makes about 2½ cups

⅓ cup slivered almonds

½ cup stale rustic bread (cut or torn into ½-inch pieces)

1 large yellow bell pepper

1¼ pounds yellow tomatoes (2 large tomatoes)

5 tablespoons extra-virgin olive oil

2 medium garlic cloves

1 tablespoon sherry vinegar

1 teaspoon sugar

½ teaspoon smoked paprika

Sea salt and freshly ground black pepper

1. Preheat the oven to 400°F with racks in the upper and middle levels. Spread out the almonds and bread pieces on a baking sheet, place on the middle oven rack, and toast until lightly golden, 5 to 6 minutes. Transfer to a food processor and set aside.

2. Adjust the oven control to broil. Place the whole pepper and tomatoes on the same baking sheet that the almonds were toasted on. Rub the pepper and tomatoes with 1 tablespoon of the olive oil and broil on the upper oven rack, turning a few times during cooking until they are charred in parts, about 10 minutes.

3. Remove any stems and pepper seeds and transfer the peppers and tomatoes to the food processor along with the garlic, vinegar, sugar, paprika, and remaining olive oil. Process until smooth, about 3 minutes. Season to taste with salt and pepper. Use immediately or store refrigerated in an airtight container for up to 1 week.

Extra Credit

• Steam **shrimp**, red snapper, and/or mussels and transfer to a large serving bowl. Spoon the sauce over the seafood and serve with plenty of bread for sopping.

• Smear golden romesco onto toasted rustic bread slices for an immediate **tapas** dish.

• Toss into cooked **pasta** along with shredded rotisserie chicken and baby spinach leaves for a quick and healthy dinner.

• Spoon over grilled **leeks** as a colorful summer side dish.

Marinated Grilled Calamari Kebabs

Soak eight 10-inch skewers in a shallow pan of cold water for about 30 minutes before using. Rinse 1¼ pounds calamari tubes and tentacles, pat dry, and cut into 2-inch pieces.

In a medium bowl, whisk together ⅓ cup olive oil, 3 cloves thinly sliced garlic, 1 tablespoon freshly grated lemon zest, 2 tablespoons fresh lemon juice, 2 teaspoons chopped fresh oregano, 1 teaspoon chopped fresh thyme, 1 teaspoon salt, and ½ teaspoon black pepper. Add the calamari to the marinade, toss to combine, cover the bowl, and refrigerate for about 30 minutes.

Preheat a grill or grill pan to medium-high heat. Thread the calamari onto the skewers, discarding the marinade. Lightly oil the grill and grill the calamari on all sides until cooked through, 6 to 8 minutes total. Serve with a dish of the golden romesco for dipping and lemon wedges for squeezing. **Serves 4**

BUTTERNUT CURRY CASHEW CREAM

This recipe is my go-to when I want to eat healthy but still indulge in a little comfort food. So rich and thick it's almost a dip, I've dunked many a cracker in this stuff for a quick snack when I've been too lazy to cook. It's also completely vegan—shhh, don't tell. Oh and by the way, you can do this with other vegetables as well. A quick way to turn your veggies into a sauce.

Makes about 1¾ cups

½ cup raw cashews

10 ounces butternut squash, peeled, halved, seeded, and cut into 1-inch chunks (2 cups)

2 (1-inch) pieces fresh ginger

1 tablespoon extra-virgin olive oil

Sea salt

½ teaspoon mild curry powder

½ teaspoon ground cumin

Freshly ground black pepper

1. Preheat the oven to 400°F. Place the cashews in a small saucepan and cover by 2 inches cold water. Bring to a boil over high heat, about 8 minutes. Turn off the heat, cover, and let steep for about 35 minutes, until the cashews feel soft to the touch.

2. Meanwhile toss the butternut squash and ginger with the olive oil and ½ teaspoon salt. Spread out on a parchment-lined baking sheet and roast, tossing once or twice during cooking, until the butternut squash is cooked through and golden in parts, 30 to 35 minutes.

3. Drain the cashews, reserving one cup cooking liquid, and transfer to a high-powered blender or food processor along with the butternut squash mixture, the curry powder, cumin, and the reserved cup of cooking liquid. Blend on high speed for about 2 minutes, until smooth, rich, and creamy. Season to taste with more salt and pepper.

Extra Credit

• Turn the sauce into a soup by warming **vegetable broth** in a saucepan and then stirring in the cashew cream to warm through.

• Mix some of the cashew cream with rice vinegar and olive oil to make a creamy salad dressing. Try this on sturdy greens like **escarole** and/or kale that's been massaged a few minutes with olive oil and salt.

• Add some chicken broth, cut-up cooked seasoned chicken breast, and fresh herbs. Let simmer, then serve over **rice**.

• Use as a vegan alternative to mayo for a creamy **sandwich** spread.

Tofu and Root Vegetable Stew

In a large pot, heat 2 tablespoons olive oil over medium heat. Add 2 finely chopped medium cloves garlic and 1 finely chopped medium shallot and cook, stirring occasionally, until fragrant, about 1 minute. Add 3 medium peeled carrots, 1 medium peeled russet potato, 1 medium peeled parsnip, 1 medium peeled sweet potato, and 1 cup 1-inch pieces peeled rutabaga. Stir in 1½ cups trimmed and halved Brussels sprouts, 1 cup water, and 1 teaspoon salt. Bring to a simmer, cover, and cook until the vegetables are fork tender, about 10 minutes.

Remove the lid and add 1 cup green beans cut into 2-inch-long pieces. Gently stir and return the lid to the pot. Cook until the green beans are tender but still green, about 10 minutes. Stir in the cashew cream and 1 cup water and heat through.

Gently stir in 14 ounces extra-firm tofu cut into 1-inch cubes (about 2 cups) until heated through. Season to taste with salt and pepper. Serve with brown rice or another whole grain. Garnish with roughly chopped cashews and a squeeze of lime, if desired. **Serves 4**

PISTACHIO CRÈME

Word seems to have gotten around that we love pistachios in my household. As a result, every year around the holidays we receive multiple large bags of the roasted, salted, in-the-shell variety—about half a year's worth (no complaints here—keep 'em coming). While this kind of pistachio is ideal for snacking, for cooking purposes I often prefer to use raw nuts. You can generally find raw shelled pistachios in the bulk aisle. They're on the expensive side, but you can buy only the amount you need. This rich and creamy savory sauce has just the right amount of pistachio flavor, and the airy texture creates a pillowy platform for anything from seafood to chicken to sit upon. It also makes a great vegan dip for crudités.

Makes about 1 cup

¾ cup raw shelled pistachio nuts

2 tablespoons canola oil

2 teaspoons sugar

1½ teaspoons white wine vinegar

Sea salt and freshly ground black pepper

1. Place the pistachios in a high-powered blender along with 1 cup boiling water. Let sit until the nuts begin to soften slightly, about 30 minutes.

2. Add the oil, sugar, and vinegar and blend on high until smooth. Season to taste with salt and pepper. Use immediately or store refrigerated in an airtight container for up to 1 week.

Should you buy pistachios in the shell or shelled? Labor intensiveness notwithstanding, I'm a strong proponent of the former; you're more likely to end up with fresher-tasting, crunchier nuts.

Extra Credit

● Serve roasted sliced chicken breast in a pool of pistachio crème topped with **diced mango**, with coconut rice on the side. Toss with pasta, cooked shrimp, and asparagus for a satisfying meal.

● Pan-fry some **eggplant** slices till browned (breaded if you like), then top with a dollop of pistachio crème, fresh mint, pomegranate seeds, and lemon zest for a tasty starter.

● Cut **pita bread** into triangles. Drizzle lightly with olive oil and sprinkle with sea salt, cumin, paprika, and pepper. Bake at 400°F until crisp, then sprinkle with a bit of sumac. Serve along with the sauce as a dip.

Crispy Salmon with Pea Greens

Use paper towels to pat the skin dry on four 6-ounce pieces of center-cut salmon (about 1¼ inches thick). Season all over with salt and pepper.

Heat a large cast-iron skillet over medium-high heat. When very hot, add 2 tablespoons canola oil and swirl to coat the pan. Place the salmon, skin side down, in the pan and cook without moving until the skin becomes golden brown and crisp, about 5 minutes. Flip the fillets and continue to cook until just cooked through, 3 to 4 minutes.

Meanwhile, heat 1 tablespoon olive oil and 1 tablespoon unsalted butter in a large high-sided skillet over medium heat. Add 2 cups shelled peas to the skillet and cook until warmed through, about 4 minutes. Add in 3 cups packed pea shoots and toss until just wilted, 2 to 3 minutes. Add 1 tablespoon fresh lemon juice to the pan, then season to taste with salt and pepper.

Use a spoon to spread ¼ cup of the pistachio crème onto the center of each of four plates. Top each with the pea greens and one salmon fillet, skin side up. Garnish with chopped pistachios, if desired. Serve immediately. **Serves 4**

Spicy

The Mother Chili

To the uninitiated, cooking with dried chile peppers may seem daunting. Gazing at the shriveled peppers in the package, you may ask, how in the world can these become a sauce? But once revived with a dip in a hot water bath and whizzed in a blender, the chiles undergo a miraculous transformation that makes the basis of this wonderfully silky sauce. Fresh and roasted chiles have their places, but nothing matches the flavor intensity of dried chiles. Chili sauce of course has a million traditional uses within Mexican cuisine (see opposite for a few). But try it in other situations, too: Drizzle it on grilled sliced steak. Sauté shrimp in the chili, then use that to top cooked stone-ground grits. Or, fold a little into cooked long-grain rice and top with sour cream and chives for a side dish with extra zip.

Makes about 1⅔ cups

4 mild to medium-hot dried chiles, such as ancho, Anaheim, or mulato

½ cup chopped white onion

2 cloves garlic, peeled

4 teaspoons agave nectar, or brown sugar

2 tablespoons canola oil

⅔ cup low-sodium chicken broth, vegetable broth, or water

2 teaspoons red wine vinegar

Sea salt

1. Cut the stems from the chiles. Remove the seeds and roughly chop or tear the chiles. Place them in the bowl of a blender or food processor along with 1 cup boiling water. Cover and let stand until softened, about 10 minutes.

2. Add the onion, garlic, and agave and blend until smooth.

3. In a medium saucepan, heat the oil over medium-high heat until shimmering. Add the chile mixture and stir to combine. Pour in the broth. Bring to a simmer and cook, stirring occasionally, until thickened, about 8 minutes. Remove from the heat and stir in the vinegar. Season to taste with salt. Serve warm or room temperature. The sauce will keep refrigerated in an airtight container for up to 1 week.

Mix It Up

Customize the mother sauce to your taste, and to use in different ways.

Creamy Lime Chili

Stir in 2 teaspoons lime zest, 1 tablespoon fresh lime juice, and ½ cup sour cream.

Sweet & Smoky Chili

Stir in 1 teaspoon canned chipotles in adobo sauce, 1 teaspoon smoked paprika, and 1 tablespoon honey.

Harissa Chili

Stir in 1½ teaspoons ground coriander, 2 teaspoons ground caraway, and 2 teaspoons ground cumin.

Corn & Cilantro Chili

Stir in 1 cup fresh corn, 3 tablespoons chopped fresh cilantro, and 1 teaspoon chopped fresh oregano.

Extra Credit

● For a party, slice a **quesadilla** into wedges on a plate. Serve with the chili sauce in a ramekin in the center for dunking. Or, pour some over tortilla chips on a baking sheet, top with grated cheese, and bake— insta-nachos!

● Wrap warmed tortillas around a filling of your choice, then bathe them in this chili sauce and bake until bubbling— **enchilada** night.

● For quick **chilaquiles**: Heat the sauce in a frying pan. Add a few large handfuls of tortilla chips and toss until the chips are well coated and start to soften slightly. Top with fried eggs and grated cheese.

● Simmer a pound of lamb stew meat in the harissa chili until tender, adding water as needed to keep the meat almost submerged. Stir in a drained can of chickpeas. Serve with couscous or warmed tortillas for a **Mexi-Moroccan dinner**.

KOREAN BARBECUE

When I lived in LA, which has one of the largest Koreatowns in the U.S., one of my favorite things to eat out was Korean barbecue, or bulgogi. I discovered that what divides the commonplace from the exquisite is the quality of the sauce in which the meat or vegetables are marinated. While some bulgogi sauces incorporate raw onion and garlic that is then cooked along with the meat, this recipe requires precooking the aromatics. This way you're not limited to using it as a marinade; you can also simply drizzle it over any cooked meat or seafood such as shrimp.

Makes about 2 cups

2 tablespoons canola oil

½ cup grated yellow onion

4 medium cloves garlic, finely chopped

2 tablespoons finely chopped jalapeño

2 teaspoons grated fresh ginger

½ cup chopped scallions, white and light green parts only

1 cup ripe but firm Asian pear or Bosc pear, peeled and grated

6 tablespoons low-sodium soy sauce

¼ cup rice wine or sake

¼ cup mirin

¼ cup toasted sesame oil

¼ cup sugar

4 teaspoons gochujang

4 teaspoons fish sauce

1. Heat the oil in a medium saucepan over medium-low heat. Add the onion, cover, and cook until very soft, about 5 minutes.

2. Remove the lid and add the garlic, jalapeño, ginger, scallions, and pear and stir to combine. Raise the heat to medium and cook, stirring occasionally, until the pear softens, about 5 minutes.

3. Add the soy sauce, wine, mirin, sesame oil, sugar, and gochujang, stir to combine, and bring to a simmer, about 3 minutes. Pour into a food processor and process until smooth, about 2 minutes. Stir in the fish sauce. Let cool to room temperature before using as a marinade. Store refrigerated in an airtight container for up to 1 week.

Some bulgogi sauces are pretty mild, but mine has a kick due to the addition of jalapeño and gochujang, a fermented chili paste.

Extra Credit

- How about **baked beans** with a Korean twist for your next barbecue or picnic: Simmer (or bake) white beans in the sauce until thick and sticky.

- Whisk rice vinegar and canola oil with a few tablespoons of bulgogi to turn it into a salad dressing. Try this with shredded **daikon** for a kimchi-like starter.

- Grill or broil **shiitake mushrooms**, then drape with this sauce. Cut into slices and serve as an appetizer.

- Brush **grilled pork tenderloin** with the sauce, then slice thinly across the grain. Serve in butter lettuce leaves with steamed cooled rice and drizzle with the sauce.

Beef and Kale Noodle Bowls

Wrap 1 pound boneless beef rib-eye in parchment paper or plastic wrap and place in the freezer for 1 to 2 hours, until just firm to the touch. Remove the parchment paper and slice the meat across the grain into long, thin strips, about $\frac{1}{16}$ inch thick. (Alternatively, to save time, check your local Asian market for pre-sliced rib-eye options.) Place the meat in a large bowl along with 3 peeled medium carrots cut into very thin matchsticks. Pour 1½ cups Korean barbecue into the bowl with the beef and carrots. Toss to coat, cover, and refrigerate for at least 30 minutes or overnight.

Cook 8 ounces Asian noodles such as Korean guksu or Japanese udon according to package directions. Run under cold water, then divide among four bowls.

Heat 1 tablespoon canola oil in a large skillet over medium-high heat. Add half the beef and cook, stirring occasionally, until just cooked through, about 5 minutes. Transfer the meat to two of the bowls. Repeat the process with the remaining beef.

Wipe out the skillet, then add 2 more tablespoons canola oil, 6 loosely packed cups chopped lacinato kale, and 2 tablespoons toasted sesame oil and season to taste with salt. Use tongs to occasionally toss the kale over medium-high heat until it is just wilted, about 4 minutes. Divide the kale among the bowls with the beef and noodles. Sprinkle each bowl with toasted sesame seeds and serve immediately. **Serves 4**

NEW MEXICAN RED CHILE

Love at first dip. That's how I'd describe my initial encounter with New Mexico–style chile sauce. I was visiting my brother and future sister-in-law in Albuquerque and whenever we went to a restaurant, the same question popped up: do you want red or green chile with that? I couldn't believe the flavor these sauces added to just about every dish. I love this chile on eggs, hashed brown potatoes, and even shrimp.

Makes about 1⅔ cups

6 to 8 dried New Mexican red chiles

1 tablespoon canola oil

1 tablespoon unsalted butter

½ cup chopped white onion

2 medium cloves garlic, finely chopped

½ teaspoon ground cumin

½ teaspoon dried oregano

2 tablespoons all-purpose flour or gluten-free flour mix

1½ cups low sodium-chicken or vegetable broth

1 teaspoon honey

Sea salt and freshly ground black pepper

1. Remove the stems from the chiles, then rip them up into small pieces. You should have about 1 cup.

2. Warm the oil and butter in a medium saucepan over medium heat. Add the chiles and onion and cook until the onion is translucent, about 2 minutes. Add the garlic, cumin, and oregano. Cook, stirring constantly, until fragrant, about 1 minute. Stir in the flour and continue to cook for about 1 minute. Add the broth and bring to a simmer. Let cook, stirring occasionally, until the chiles have softened and the mixture thickens, about 12 minutes total.

3. Transfer to a high-powered blender or food processor along with the honey. Remove the middle part of the lid of the blender, if using, and cover with a paper towel before blending to let the steam escape. Season to taste with salt and pepper. Serve warm or room temperature. Store refrigerated in an airtight container for up to 1 week.

Extra Credit

● Mix with mayo and use as a creamy spread for **sandwiches**, especially those featuring turkey.

● For a spicier green riff: substitute 1 cup torn dried Hatch green chiles for the red variety. Serve with a spinach and queso fresco **omelette** or add a dollop to chicken and rice soup.

● Smear a large warm flour tortilla with the chile, then top with refried beans, corn, rice, chopped tomatoes, avocado, sour cream, and a squirt of lime. Roll up into the **burrito** of your dreams.

● Drizzle over a **taco** in place of salsa, or bathe tortillas in it when making enchiladas.

Fried Egg Tostadas

Preheat the oven to 400°F. Line a baking sheet with parchment paper. Place four 5-inch-diameter corn tortillas on the prepared pan and spread each with 3 tablespoons refried beans and 3 tablespoons Mexican shredded cheese blend. Bake until the cheese has melted and the tortillas are crisp, 12 to 15 minutes.

Meanwhile, heat 2 tablespoons canola oil in a large cast-iron skillet over medium-high heat. Crack 4 large eggs into the skillet and season each with some salt and pepper. Cover with a lid and cook until the egg whites are set but the yolks are still runny, 6 to 8 minutes.

Transfer the tortillas to a plate and top with a fried egg, sliced avocado, cilantro sprigs, and a drizzle of New Mexican red chile. Serve immediately.
Serves 4

GREEN COCONUT CURRY

In our household, we used to have a once-weekly ritual of ordering in Thai green curry. Then one day our local joint was closed, and I decided to whip up my own. Curry is not a flavor in itself but a variable blend of aromatics and spices. My green curry relies slightly more on lemongrass than the typical Thai restaurant's, and it's a bit milder. If you want extra heat, just add more chile. Toss this on any cooked protein and/or vegetables for a dinner you're sure to start craving weekly.

Makes about 2 cups

1 (3-inch) piece fresh lemongrass, finely chopped

½ to 1 green Thai or Anaheim chile, stemmed

1 tablespoon finely chopped fresh ginger

½ cup packed fresh basil leaves

¼ cup packed fresh cilantro

Half of 1 medium shallot, chopped

2 medium cloves garlic

2 teaspoons fresh chopped kaffir lime leaves

½ teaspoon ground coriander

½ teaspoon ground cumin

¼ teaspoon ground cardamom

4 teaspoons shrimp paste

3 tablespoons canola oil

1½ cups coconut milk

2 teaspoons palm sugar or dark brown sugar

4 teaspoons fish sauce

2 teaspoons fresh lime juice

1. In a food processor, combine the lemongrass, chiles, ginger, basil, cilantro, shallot, garlic, kaffir lime leaves, coriander, cumin, and cardamom and pulse about 50 times, until finely chopped. Add the shrimp paste and 2 tablespoons of the oil and process until a paste forms.

2. In a medium saucepan, heat the remaining 1 tablespoon oil over medium heat. Add the green curry paste and stir constantly until simmering and heated through, about 3 minutes. Stir in the coconut milk, sugar, and fish sauce. Bring to a simmer, about 4 minutes, and cook until the flavors develop, about 5 minutes. Turn off the heat and stir in the lime juice. Use immediately or store refrigerated in an airtight container for up to 1 week.

Extra Credit

● Add noodles and shrimp, chicken, or tofu to the sauce for an easy dreamy **noodle stew**.

● Add 1 to 2 cups chicken or vegetable stock and a squeeze or two more fresh lime juice to make a "green" soup base for **gai tom ka soup**.

● Drizzle green coconut curry over cooked beef or **chicken skewers**, or use as a marinade for skewered meat before grilling.

● Revive old **leftover rice** by simmering it in this curry; top with meat, vegetables, and fresh herbs.

Sizzling Thai Mussels

Scrub 4 pounds fresh mussels well and cut off the beards. In a large bowl, toss the mussels in 1 tablespoon canola oil. Heat a large tall pot with a lid over medium-high heat. When very hot, add the mussels. Use a long spoon to stir a few times as they sizzle in the pot. Add the green coconut curry, reduce the heat to medium, stir to combine, and cover with the lid. Cook, stirring once or twice, until the mussels have opened, 10 to 12 minutes.

Transfer the mussels and sauce to a serving dish, discarding any unopened mussels. Garnish with fresh torn basil leaves. Serve immediately.
Serves 4

ETHIOPIAN BERBERE SAUCE

If you haven't yet tried the vibrant and highly flavorful cuisine of Ethiopia, I'd urge you to seek it out. The basis of most meals, is a tangy, spongy flatbread called injera. Many different types of stewed dishes are placed in little piles atop the bread. Diners tear off pieces of injera to scoop up the meats and vegetables—utensil-free eating. This spicy sauce is my way of making the most of berbere, the famous dried spice mix that comes from Ethiopia. Berbere brings new life to any cooked vegetable or as a marinade for beef or chicken. I also use it as a condiment for grilled meats and bread.

Makes about 1¼ cups

1 teaspoon fenugreek seeds

¼ teaspoon ground allspice

2 pods green cardamom

⅛ teaspoon freshly grated nutmeg

⅛ teaspoon ground cinnamon

¼ teaspoon cayenne pepper

½ teaspoon black peppercorns

3 tablespoons extra-virgin olive oil

1 medium onion, finely chopped

2 tablespoons finely chopped fresh ginger

1 tablespoon finely chopped fresh turmeric or 1 teaspoon ground turmeric

4 cloves garlic, finely chopped

½ cup dry red wine

½ cup finely chopped fresh cilantro

1 teaspoon red wine vinegar

1 teaspoon sea salt

1. Using a mortar and pestle or a spice grinder, grind the fenugreek, allspice, cardamom, nutmeg, cinnamon, cayenne pepper, and black peppercorns together and set aside.

2. Heat the oil in a medium saucepan over medium heat. Add the onion, ginger, and turmeric and cook, stirring occasionally until the onion is very soft, about 15 minutes.

3. Add the garlic and dried spice mixture and cook until fragrant, about 1 minute, then pour in the wine and cook until almost completely evaporated, about 4 minutes. Turn the heat off and stir in the cilantro, vinegar, and salt. Serve warm or room temperature. Store in an airtight container in the refrigerator for up to 1 week.

Extra Credit

- Stir a bit of sauce into rice and cooked crumbled ground beef, then use as a filling for baked **stuffed red peppers**.

- Stir the sauce into cooked **lentils** and serve with rice, or if you have it, injera.

- Amp up a classic supper of the American South: Stir the sauce into stewed **collard greens** and serve with cornbread for dunking.

- Spread a bit of sauce onto toasted rustic bread, then top with **sliced roast beef**, avocado, tomato, microgreens, and another piece of toasted rustic bread.

Winter Squash and Chickpea Stew

Heat ¼ cup extra-virgin olive oil in a large high-sided skillet over medium-high heat. Add 5 cups 1-inch pieces of winter squash (from either 1 small butternut, kabocha, or acorn). Cook, stirring occasionally, until tender and golden brown in parts, about 20 minutes.

Add 3 cups drained cooked chickpeas and 1 teaspoon salt and cook, stirring occasionally, until the chickpeas are warmed through, about 3 minutes. Stir in ¼ cup tomato paste until completely combined, then stir in 1 batch Ethiopian berbere and 1 cup water, reduce the heat to medium-low, and simmer to develop the flavors, about 3 minutes.

Season to taste with more salt. Serve warm or room temperature with a dollop of whole-milk yogurt, a handful of fresh cilantro, and pita, naan bread, or injera if you can find it in a specialty shop. **Serves 4**

When using fresh herbs, don't discount the stems; they have tons of flavor. If they're tender, chop and add along with the leaves to your sauces and other recipes. If they're woodier, save them in a large resealable container in the freezer, to throw into stock.

CHARRED POBLANO AND TOMATILLO MOJO

This lovable mutt of a recipe incorporates elements of both Mexican, Caribbean, and Southwestern cooking. For a sauce with such complexity (sweet, tart, spicy, creamy, salty all in one!) it is relatively simple to make. A few brief notes on ingredients: The tomatillo, a diminutive and tart relative of the tomato that you eat when still green, has a thin papery husk you must remove. While poblano peppers generally range from mild to medium heat, once in a while you end up with a spicy one. If you want even more heat, add a jalapeño to the mix when broiling the vegetables. If you want more creaminess, stir in some sour cream. My instinct is to use this sauce on tacos, but don't let that stop you from experimenting with other options.

Makes about 3 cups

2 poblano peppers

4 medium tomatillos, husks peeled

1 medium white onion, peeled, cut into quarters

3 cloves garlic, peels on

2 tablespoons canola oil

1 avocado, pitted and peeled

3 tablespoons fresh lime juice

½ cup chopped fresh cilantro

Sea salt

1. Preheat the oven to broil with a rack position at the highest level. Toss the poblanos, tomatillos, onion, and garlic in the oil and spread out on a baking sheet. Broil the vegetables, tossing a few times during the process, until blistered all over, 8 to 10 minutes.

2. Transfer just the poblanos to a medium bowl. Cover the bowl with plastic wrap and steam the peppers for about 10 minutes. Peel and seed the poblanos and transfer them to a food processor along with the tomatillos, onion, peeled garlic, and avocado. Pulse until smooth. Add the lime juice, cilantro, and salt to taste and pulse to combine. Store refrigerated in an airtight container for up to 1 week.

Extra Credit

● How about green eggs (ham optional)? Serve the mojo over **fried eggs** on toast for a real wake-up breakfast.

● For a real island-style feast, grill some **red snapper** fillets, then spoon this sauce on top. Serve with the smashed plantains and/or black beans and rice on the side.

● Tired of the same-old guacamole? This sauce will turn any bag of **chips** into a party.

● Drizzle over **fried eggplant** (see page 59), or almost any fried veggie really.

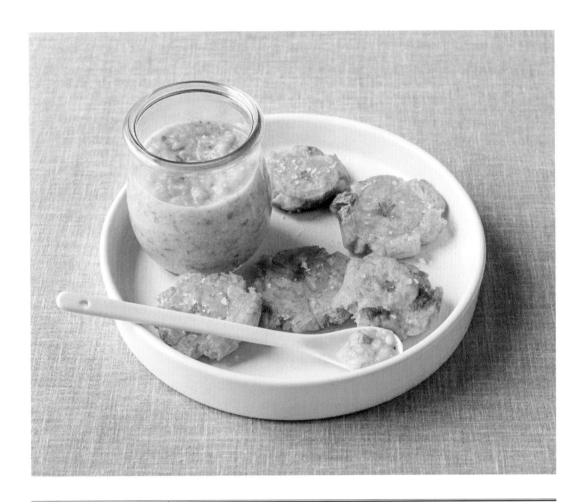

Crispy Smashed Plantains

Cut the ends off each of 3 green plantains. Use a knife to make a vertical slit down each one, and then carefully peel the plantains and slice crosswise into 1-inch-thick slices.

Pour 1 inch of canola oil into a large high-sided skillet and heat over medium-high heat until a deep-fry thermometer reads 360°F. Fry the plantains in batches (turning over once halfway through cooking) until lightly golden, about 4 minutes per batch. Use a slotted spoon to transfer the plantains to a paper towel–lined baking sheet. Turn off the heat.

Use a heavy metal spatula or meat mallet to smash the plantains to ¼-inch thickness. Reheat the oil to 360°F. Fry the plantains again in batches until dark golden and crisp, about 4 minutes. Return to the paper towel–lined baking sheet and immediately sprinkle with salt. Dip the plantains in the charred poblano and tomatillo mojo and serve immediately. **Serves 4**

EGGPLANT ZHOUG

This bright green Middle Eastern sauce, especially popular in Yemen and Israel, is summertime in a bowl, often served atop a pita sandwich or shawarma. Typically, zhoug is a smooth and spicy pesto-like condiment. Mine is chunkier since it uses chopped grilled eggplant as the base. When mixed with hot peppers, fresh herbs, olive oil, and spices, it livens up toast or crackers, gives sandwiches a flavor boost, and adds an exotic kick to a grilled steak.

Makes about 2 cups

1¼ pounds eggplant, peeled and sliced crosswise into ¼-inch-thick rounds

2 tablespoons plus ¼ cup extra-virgin olive oil

1 to 2 jalapeños, stems removed

1 packed cup fresh cilantro leaves and stems

1 packed cup fresh flat-leaf parsley leaves and stems

¼ cup fresh mint leaves

1 medium clove garlic, peeled

½ teaspoon ground coriander

½ teaspoon ground cumin

4 teaspoons red wine vinegar

1 teaspoon dark brown sugar

Sea salt and freshly ground black pepper

1. Preheat a grill or grill pan to medium-high heat. Brush the eggplant with 2 tablespoons of the olive oil. Lightly oil the grill and cook the eggplant in batches for 6 to 8 minutes, flipping halfway through cooking, until grill marks form on both sides. Transfer the eggplant to a cutting board, roughly chop into approximately ¼-inch pieces, and place in a medium bowl.

2. In the bowl of a food processor, combine the jalapeños, cilantro, parsley, mint, garlic, coriander, cumin, vinegar, sugar, and remaining ¼ cup olive oil and pulse about 30 times, until finely chopped. Add to the bowl with the eggplant and gently stir to combine. Season to taste with salt and pepper. Store refrigerated in an airtight container for up to 5 days.

Extra Credit

• Spoon onto toasted flatbread for a Middle Eastern twist on **bruschetta** and serve with olives.

• Stir eggplant zhoug into **cold pasta** for a pasta salad that will transport you to the Mediterranean.

• Top a round of **pizza** dough with cheese and thawed frozen artichoke hearts. Bake in a hot oven until crispy, then spoon the eggplant zhoug on top.

• Make a fabulous **veggie sandwich** starting with good-quality multigrain bread, then top with eggplant zhoug, tahini sauce (page 88), fresh basil, tomato slices, roasted red peppers, shredded carrots, and chopped lettuce.

Spiced Socca with Feta

In a medium bowl, whisk together ¾ cup chickpea flour, ¾ teaspoon salt, ½ teaspoon black pepper, ¼ teaspoon smoked paprika, and ½ teaspoon ground coriander. Whisk in ¾ cup warm water and 2 tablespoons extra-virgin olive oil until smooth. The batter should be the consistency of heavy cream. Cover the bowl with plastic wrap and let sit for about 1 hour.

Preheat the oven to 500°F. Place a 10-inch cast-iron skillet in the oven to heat. Remove from the oven once hot, add 2 tablespoons olive oil to the pan, and swirl to coat. Pour the batter into the pan and return to the oven. Cook until the socca is firm and set and the edges are golden brown, 12 to 15 minutes.

Turn out the socca onto a cutting board and cut into wedges. Spoon some of the eggplant zhoug over the top and sprinkle with 3 tablespoons crumbled feta and a bit of za'atar spice. Serve immediately. **Serves 4**

QUICK JERK

This recipe is inspired by an airport meal, believe it or not. My husband and I were taking a trip to the Caribbean island of Tortola—with multiple stops thanks to a shoestring budget. After traveling all day, we finally arrived, parched and starving, at what might be called an airport, although it was really little more than a strip of land between two huge gorgeous mountains overlooking the bright aqua ocean. We stumbled over to the café—a straw-thatched cottage with outdoor seats and many cats and goats milling around. The menu was simple . . . jerk chicken, jerk goat, and a couple side dishes. I went with the chicken (the goats staring at us made it an easy choice). The dish that arrived was revelatory: freshly grilled, deliciously charred, flavorful to the bone, and so juicy yet crisp on the exterior. It was the best meal of our entire trip, despite many other good ones. I have thought about that meal many times since, though it was almost ten years ago. My version of the jerk sauce—a pretty fair approximation if I may say so—uses lots of aromatics including freshly grated nutmeg. A purist would insist on chopping by hand but this quick jerk uses the help of a food processor to speed things along. I like to use it as a marinade or simmer it and spoon it on top of grilled seafood or meat.

Makes about 1⅓ cups

4 scallions, chopped (about 1 cup)

1 cup chopped white onion

4 teaspoons chopped fresh ginger

2 medium cloves garlic, peeled

½ to 1 Scotch bonnet chile or jalapeño

1 tablespoon fresh thyme leaves

4 teaspoons tomato paste

2 tablespoons dark brown sugar

2 tablespoons lime zest (from 2 limes)

1½ teaspoons ground allspice

½ teaspoon freshly grated nutmeg

5 tablespoons fresh lime juice

1 tablespoon canola oil

1½ teaspoons sea salt

½ teaspoon freshly ground black pepper

Place all of the ingredients in a food processor and process for about 2 minutes, scraping down the sides of the bowl, if necessary, until a paste forms. Use immediately or store refrigerated in an airtight container for up to 2 weeks.

Extra Credit

● Jerk is really just barbecue sauce, Caribbean style. Use it anywhere you might use barbecue sauce, such as atop a **burger**.

● For a quick dip, beat 2 to 3 tablespoons quick jerk into ½ cup cream cheese and ¼ cup sour cream and stir in chopped scallions. Use as a **dip** for any raw vegetables and/or crackers.

● Brush some onto **corn on the cob** right before it goes on the grill.

● For a vegetarian take on jerk, stew canned **jackfruit** in some of the sauce until the flavors marry. Serve with rice and peas.

Double Jerk Chicken Wings

Place 24 party-style wings (about 2¾ pounds) in a large resealable bag with 1 cup of the quick jerk. Press out the air from the bag, seal, and use your hands to press and move the bag around to coat the wings in the sauce. Let marinate in the refrigerator for at least 1 hour.

Preheat the oven to 475°F. Transfer the chicken wings to a large bowl and toss with 3 tablespoons all-purpose flour and ½ teaspoon salt. Arrange the wings on an oil-rubbed parchment-lined baking sheet and bake, flipping once halfway through cooking, until they are browned in parts, cooked through, and crisp, 35 to 40 minutes.

Meanwhile, place the remaining ⅓ cup jerk sauce and ½ cup water in a small saucepan over medium heat. Bring to a simmer and cook until the mixture has thickened, about 15 minutes. Remove the chicken from the oven and brush the cooked sauce over the top. Transfer the wings to a serving platter and garnish with fresh chopped scallions. Serve immediately. **Serves 4**

KIMCHI BUTTER

This sauce has only four ingredients but packs a flavor wallop nonetheless, thanks to its two primary ingredients, kimchi and koji (see Notes). Both of these products can usually be found at Asian markets or purchased online. If you can't find koji, try substituting sweet white miso, which has a similar flavor. While kimchi is typically eaten cold, here I've warmed it and added butter to mellow out the intensity, and the richness of the koji further rounds out the flavor. I like eating this sauce stirred straight into steamed white or brown rice. It's also superb as a topping for starchy sides, as in the recipe opposite.

Makes about ¾ cup

1 tablespoon unsalted butter, plus 4 tablespoons cold unsalted butter, cut into small pieces

¾ cup mild to medium kimchi, chopped

2 teaspoons shio rice koji or sweet white miso

½ teaspoon rice vinegar

Melt 1 tablespoon of the butter in a medium saucepan over medium heat. Add the kimchi and cook until heated through, about 3 minutes. Stir in the shio koji and vinegar and turn off the heat. Whisk in the remaining 4 tablespoons cold butter, a little at a time, until the sauce thickens. Serve immediately.

Kimchi, as you may know, is a Korean fermented condiment made of fermented raw vegetables (usually Napa cabbage), garlic, ginger, chiles, salt, and vinegar. I absolutely love the flavor and texture and heat.

As for koji (full name shio koji), this is a fermented white paste made of malted rice, salt, and water, which adds a rich umami flavor that enhances anything it touches.

Extra Credit

● Use in place of butter for a more flavorful **baked potato** topper to serve alongside a classic steak meal.

● Stir kimchi butter into rice or any **whole grain** and top with a fried egg and some shredded toasted seaweed for a comforting meal.

● Stir kimchi butter into sautéed mixed vegetables such as kale, chopped sweet potatoes, and **kohlrabi** and serve on top of buckwheat soba noodles with a splash of soy sauce and sesame oil.

● Spoon onto a store-bought puffed **rice cake** for a flavorful snack.

Seoul Crispy Rice Cakes

In a large bowl, combine 2 cups cooked and cooled steamed white rice, ½ cup shredded raw carrot, ½ cup shredded raw zucchini, ¼ cup chopped scallions, 2 teaspoons toasted sesame oil, 2 teaspoons low-sodium soy sauce, 1 tablespoon glutinous rice flour (mochiko), and ½ teaspoon salt. Beat 1 large egg in a small bowl and stir it into the rice mixture. Form the rice mixture into eight 2½-inch-diameter cakes. (The mixture will feel loose.) Place the patties on a parchment-lined baking sheet and refrigerate for 1 hour, or until firm.

Heat 2 tablespoons canola oil in a large high-sided skillet over medium-high heat. Once shimmering, add the rice cakes in batches. Cook, flipping once during the cooking process, until golden brown and crispy on both sides, about 4 minutes total per batch. Drain on a paper towel–lined plate, then transfer to plates and spoon kimchi butter over the top. Serve immediately. **Serves 2 to 4**

Chunky

The Mother Salsa

Salsa simply means "sauce" in Spanish. So it makes sense that Mexican salsas vary considerably in texture and ingredients. In general, though, our north-of-the-border definition of salsa revolves around a base of fresh veggies or fruits, diced or blended, with some form of heat, citrus or vinegar, plus aromatics and salt. Here I've concentrated on the fresh and chunky variety (if you are a fan of blended hot sauces, take a look at the Mother Chili on page 108). Pretty much any of these work as a chip dip, burrito component, or taco topper.

Makes about 2 cups

1½ cups chopped ripe tomatoes

½ cup chopped white onion

¼ cup chopped fresh cilantro

2 tablespoons fresh lime juice

1 tablespoon seeded and finely chopped jalapeño pepper

Sea salt

Place the tomatoes, onion, cilantro, lime juice, and jalapeño in a medium bowl and stir to combine. Season to taste with salt. Let sit at room temperature for up to 30 minutes for the flavors to develop. Use right away or store refrigerated in an airtight container for up to 3 days.

Mix It Up

Customize the mother sauce to your taste, and to use in different ways.

Pineapple & Chipotle Salsa

Replace the tomatoes with 1½ cups chopped fresh pineapple. Replace the jalapeño with 1 tablespoon chopped chipotles in adobo.

Corn & Roasted Garlic Salsa

Stir in ½ cup cooked fresh corn kernels, 6 chopped roasted garlic cloves (see Note), and ½ teaspoon ground coriander.

Avocado & Mango Salsa

Replace the tomato with 1 cup chopped fresh mango and stir in ½ cup chopped fresh avocado and ½ teaspoon chili powder just before serving.

Apple & Radish Salsa

Replace the tomatoes with 1 cup chopped Granny Smith apple and ½ cup chopped radishes, and replace the white onion with ½ cup chopped red onion.

Note: To roast garlic: Preheat the oven to 400°F. Cut about ½ inch off the top of one head of garlic, exposing a little of the cloves, and place on a piece of foil on a baking sheet. Pour 2 tablespoons extra-virgin olive oil over the top of the garlic and then wrap in the foil. Roast until the garlic cloves are very tender and slightly golden, 45 to 50 minutes.

Extra Credit

● For a quick snack, fill half of a **pitted avocado** with any one of the salsas (except the avocado one). Eat with a spoon.

● Use the pineapple and chipotle or avocado and mango variations to top **grilled fish** or shrimp.

● Beautifully accessorize **gazpacho** or a chilled avocado soup with any of these salsas.

● Make a weekday pork chop dinner special by serving with the apple and radish salsa, maybe with some **polenta** or grits on the side.

BACON AND CHIVE GALLIMAUFRY

Gallimaufry means a hodgepodge, confused medley, ragout, or hash. Its etymology seems rooted in old French words for "have fun" and eat copious quantities. I came up with this recipe because of, well, bacon. The other ingredients complement the bacon's natural richness, adding notes of sweetness and acidity. It is great just slapped onto some bread or used as a topper for a creamy winter squash or root vegetable soup. The uses are endless if you are craving bacon, which, let's face it, you probably are.

Makes about ⅔ cup

4 slices thick-cut bacon, coarsely chopped

1 medium shallot, finely chopped

¼ cup apple cider

3 tablespoons apple cider vinegar

1 teaspoon dark brown sugar

2 tablespoons cold unsalted butter, cut into small cubes

3 tablespoons snipped fresh chives

Sea salt and freshly ground black pepper

1. Cook the bacon in a medium cast-iron or heavy-bottomed skillet over medium heat, stirring occasionally, until fat has rendered and the bacon is crisp. Use a slotted spoon to transfer the bacon to a paper towel–lined plate. Reserve the fat in the skillet.

2. Add the shallot to the skillet and cook, stirring occasionally, until it just begins to soften, about 3 minutes. Add the cider, vinegar, and brown sugar and cook until reduced by half, about 4 minutes. Whisk in the butter, a few pieces at a time, until it melts and the sauce takes on a glossy consistency. Stir in the bacon and chives and season to taste with salt and pepper. Use immediately.

Extra Credit

• This makes a lovely warm dressing for any number of sturdy **salad greens**, such as spinach, arugula, frisée, or kale.

• Spoon gallimaufry over **cooked scallops**, shrimp, or clams to launch them into the flavor stratosphere.

• Spread on a piece of **toast** and top with a fried egg for a sophisticated twist on bacon and eggs.

• If you want something a little more virtuous to balance out all the butter and bacon, toss this sauce with some roasted **cauliflower florets**.

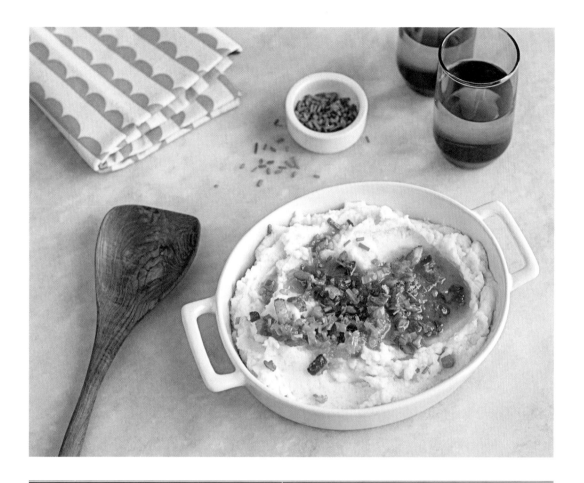

Whipped Turnip Mashed Potatoes

Peel 1 pound turnips and 2 pounds russet potatoes. Cut both into 1½-inch pieces and place in a large pot. Pour in enough cold water to cover the potatoes and turnips by 2 inches. Season with 2 tablespoons salt. Bring the water to a boil over high heat, about 15 minutes. Continue to boil until the root vegetables are fork tender, about 8 minutes. Drain and return to the pot. Use a ricer or potato masher to mash them together.

In a separate small saucepan, combine ⅔ cup heavy cream, 3 tablespoons unsalted butter,

⅓ cup chicken or vegetable broth, 1 dried bay leaf, and 3 sprigs fresh thyme. Bring to a boil over medium heat and continue to cook until the flavors develop, about 3 more minutes. Discard the bay leaf and thyme and pour the liquid over the root vegetable mixture.

Use a spoon to combine and season to taste with salt. Transfer the turnip potatoes to a serving dish and pour the bacon and chive gallimaufry over the top. Serve immediately. **Serves 4**

SALSA AL ZUCCHINI

From my days in cooking school, I remember a chef instructor discussing the difference between French and Italian cuisines. In French cuisine, the raw ingredients tend to get manipulated and transformed into something new and wonderful—a silky soufflé or a wobbly terrine. Italian cooking, in contrast, seeks to showcase and emphasize the natural flavors and textures of the ingredients being used. I love both styles, but this summery recipe goes the Italian route. Briny pancetta, juicy tomatoes, and fresh zucchini shine as the key ingredients. A few notes on them: 1) If you can find them, I recommend using small zucchini in this recipe as their flavor tends to be more delicate than large late-summer zucchini, which can become woody (save these for zucchini bread). 2) The tomatoes are added at the end along with the herbs, after the heat has been turned off. This warms them through without cooking them, allowing you to maintain their fresh and juicy quality and avoid mushiness. The fresher the better. 3) The pancetta, a salty cured pork, is more of a supporting player than star in this dish—its primary purpose is to enrich the vegetables in the sauce. The end result is a coarsely chopped, rustic sauce that's great with pasta or as a topping for grilled or roast chicken.

Makes about 3½ cups

3 ounces pancetta, cut into small dice (about ¾ cup)

3 cloves garlic, peeled and thinly sliced

2 small zucchinis (about 12 ounces total), cut into ½-inch dice (about 3 cups)

2 ripe tomatoes (about 12 ounces total)

1 tablespoon balsamic vinegar

1 cup torn basil leaves

¼ cup chopped fresh parsley

Sea salt and freshly ground black pepper

1. Heat a large high-sided skillet over medium-high heat. Add the pancetta and cook, stirring occasionally, until the fat has rendered and the pancetta is crisp, 2 to 3 minutes.

2. Add the garlic to the skillet and cook, stirring occasionally, until fragrant, about 1 minute.

3. Add the zucchini and cook, stirring constantly, about 3 minutes, until crisp tender. Turn the heat off and add the tomatoes, vinegar, basil, and parsley. Toss to combine and season to taste with salt and pepper. Serve immediately.

Extra Credit

- Top **pizza** dough (store-bought or homemade) with the sauce and fresh mozzarella or Parmesan. Bake until the cheese has melted, the sauce is bubbly, and the crust is golden.

- Halve an **acorn squash** lengthwise, roast until tender, then top with this sauce for a healthy supper.

- Make a **shrimp-and-rice** Italian stir fry: After cooking the salsa in the pan, toss in some shrimp, season with salt and pepper, and cook until the shrimp is just opaque, 2 to 3 minutes. Then stir in a couple cups of pre-cooked rice and toss through until warm.

- Use as a **polenta** topping for a quick but satisfying meal.

Ricotta and Herb Gnocchi

Place 12 ounces (about 1½ cups) whole-milk ricotta in a large bowl. Add 1 large egg, ½ cup grated Parmesan cheese, 1 tablespoon extra-virgin olive oil, ¼ cup finely chopped flat-leaf parsley, 2 teaspoons chopped fresh thyme leaves, 1 teaspoon salt, and ½ teaspoon black pepper and stir to combine. Add 1¼ cups all-purpose flour and stir until a dough forms.

Turn out the dough onto a lightly floured large cutting board. Form into a ball, adding more flour if the mixture feels too sticky. Cut the ball into 4 equal pieces, then roll each into a ½-inch-thick rope. Cut crosswise into 1-inch pieces. Roll each piece off the back of the tines of a fork to make imprints. Place on a parchment-lined baking sheet.

Bring a large pot of salted water to a boil. Add half the gnocchi and cook until they have floated to the top of the pot, about 3 minutes. Repeat the process with the remaining gnocchi.

Transfer the gnocchi to the skillet with the salsa al zucchini. Add 2 tablespoons extra-virgin olive oil and toss to combine. Serve immediately, sprinkled with more Parmesan cheese, if desired. **Serves 4**

KALEIDOSCOPE CHICKPEA AND TOMATO HASH

This extra-chunky medley of a sauce was designed to appeal equally to the palate and the palette (thank you very much, I'll be appearing in Cleveland tomorrow!). It provides a colorful, painterly backdrop and a creamy, mellow richness to whatever it accompanies. Its centerpiece, the humble chickpea, brings a hit of protein and satisfying heft that, combined with a platform grain or pasta, makes for a legit entrée. This sauce is a real scene stealer, in a good way, since it brings so much to the table that you can pair it with the blandest of foods, from leftover green beans to turkey breast. Or, for a killer app, simply smother it on some thinly sliced rustic toast and top with mozzarella.

Makes about 2 cups

¼ cup extra-virgin olive oil

3 medium thinly sliced garlic cloves

1 tablespoon chopped fresh rosemary

1 tablespoon tomato paste

1 cup cooked or canned chickpeas, rinsed and drained

2 cups halved small cherry or grape tomatoes of any color

½ cup low-sodium chicken or vegetable broth

2 tablespoons chopped fresh flat-leaf parsley

Sea salt and freshly ground black pepper

1. In a large high-sided skillet, warm the olive oil and garlic over medium-low heat, stirring occasionally. When the garlic begins to look lightly golden around the edges, about 6 minutes, add the rosemary and tomato paste and stir to combine.

2. Add the chickpeas and stir gently to combine and warm through. Add the tomatoes and broth. Raise the heat to medium-high, bring to a simmer, and cook until the tomatoes have softened slightly, about 3 minutes. Stir in the parsley and season to taste with salt and pepper. Use immediately or store refrigerated in an airtight container for up to 3 days.

Extra Credit

- Fill crepes with the sauce, fold over to form triangles, top with grated **Gruyère cheese**, then bake in the oven until the cheese is melted.

- In a baking dish coated with olive oil, layer thinly sliced eggplant and zucchini with the sauce and mozzarella cheese. Cover with foil and bake until cooked through for a gluten-free, **noodle-free lasagna**.

- Fold the sauce into cooked **couscous**, maybe with some briny black olives for a main-course salad that will really sparkle at a picnic.

- Slice **focaccia** in half, spoon on the chickpea and tomato hash, top with a fried egg, and you have an exemplary sandwich.

Roast Chicken Thighs Provençal

Preheat the oven to 450°F. Pat 6 bone-in, skin-on chicken thighs dry with paper towels and season all over with salt and pepper. Heat a large cast-iron or heavy ovenproof skillet over high heat. When very hot, add 1 tablespoon canola oil and half the chicken, skin side down, to the pan. Let cook, undisturbed, until the skin is crisp and golden brown, about 4 minutes. Flip over and continue to cook until browned on all sides, about 4 more minutes.

Transfer the chicken, skin side up, to a plate. Drain the fat from the skillet and repeat with the

remaining chicken. Take the skillet off the heat and drain all the fat from the skillet.

Pour the chickpea and tomato hash into the skillet and bring to a simmer over medium heat, about 4 minutes. Place the chicken thighs on top of the sauce and transfer to the oven. Continue to roast until the thighs have an internal temperature of 165°F, 15 to 18 minutes. Remove from the oven and let rest for 5 minutes before serving. Divide among plates and top with freshly torn basil leaves.
Serves 4 as a small plate

OLD SCHOOL BROOKLYN HOT SALAD

Deep into Brooklyn, there is a fabled sandwich shop known as Defonte's. We used to make the trek for their coronary-inducing heroes, overflowing with meat, sometimes several kinds within a sandwich. One of their famous sides is a combo of pickled veggies known as "hot salad." Not really a salad, and not that hot either, this relishy sauce hearkens back to a time when Italian-American cuisine was still trying to position itself in a way that the mainstream could understand. What follows is my riff on it.

Makes about 2¼ cups

1 mild light green pepper, such as Hungarian wax

1 red bell pepper

3 cloves garlic with peels left on

3 tablespoons plus 1 teaspoon extra-virgin olive oil

½ cup pimento-stuffed green olives

½ cup pitted Kalamata olives

2 pepperoncini, stems removed

2 tablespoons drained capers

1 tablespoon red wine vinegar

½ cup chopped fresh flat-leaf parsley

1. Preheat the oven to broil with a rack on the highest level. Toss the mild green and red peppers and the garlic in 1 teaspoon of the oil and spread out on a baking sheet. Broil the vegetables, tossing a few times during the process, until blistered all over, 8 to 10 minutes. Transfer the peppers to a medium bowl, cover the bowl with plastic wrap, and steam for about 10 minutes. Peel and seed both peppers and place in the bowl of a food processor. Peel the garlic and add it to the food processor along with the olives and pepperoncini. Pulse about 15 times, until coarsely chopped. Transfer to a medium bowl.

2. Add the capers, vinegar, parsley, and remaining 3 tablespoons olive oil and stir to combine. Use immediately or refrigerate in an airtight container for up to 4 days. Bring up to room temperature about 30 minutes before using.

Extra Credit

• Sprinkle the sauce over a bowl of store-bought **hummus** and you have an appetizer worthy of a mezze platter.

• Slice an eggplant and roast until light golden. Let cool slightly. Place a spoonful of Brooklyn hot salad in the middle of each slice, roll them up, and secure with toothpicks to create **involtini**.

• Top mild, grilled fish with the old school hot salad and serve **broccolini** and blistered tomatoes alongside.

• Stir a little into canned **olive oil–packed tuna** for a great mayo-free tuna salad option.

Super Italian Hoagie

Split two 12-inch Italian loaves in half lengthwise. In a small bowl, mix ¼ cup tomato paste with 2 tablespoons olive oil. Spread on the bottom half of each loaf. Evenly spread some of the Old School Brooklyn hot salad over the tomato paste.

Top each sandwich with 2½ ounces thinly sliced mortadella, 1½ ounces thinly sliced salami, 2½ ounces thinly sliced capicola (coppa), 2½ ounces thinly sliced provolone cheese, 1 cup shredded iceburg lettuce, 1 thinly sliced ripe tomato, and 5 to 6 fresh basil leaves.

Spread a thin layer of mayo on the top half of each loaf and close the sandwiches. Slice each sandwich in half crosswise and serve immediately. **Serves 4**

QUINCE, APPLE, AND TURMERIC CHUTNEY

I first tried quince when I was on my honeymoon in coastal Uruguay. In South America the fruit most commonly appears in a Spanish preparation called membrillo, in which it's cooked into a jelly-like paste that is often served as part of a cheese course. The membrillo was deliciously tart, sticky, and sweet, acting to break the richness of all the salty and creamy cheeses. Upon my return to the United States, I immediately added quince to my flavor arsenal. Similar in shape and appearance to a pear, the quince must be cooked to be eaten; after a while on the heat its light yellow flesh turns a darker amber. The quince's core is very hard and contains inedible seeds; use a good sharp knife to carefully remove it. This chutney, which incorporates apples and fresh spices like ginger and turmeric to contrast with the quince, is perfect for any cheese plate or as a condiment for a variety of meats and sandwiches—try it mixed with mayo when used in a chicken salad sandwich.

Makes about 4 cups

1 teaspoon canola oil

1 teaspoon mustard seeds

1 teaspoon cumin seeds

1 cup chopped yellow onion

1 tablespoon finely chopped fresh ginger

2 tablespoons finely chopped fresh turmeric or 1 tablespoon ground turmeric

1 teaspoon ground coriander

½ teaspoon ground cardamom

2 large quinces, peeled, cored, and coarsely chopped

⅓ cup apple cider vinegar

½ cup packed dark brown sugar

2 apples, such as Gala or Honeycrisp, peeled, cored, and coarsely chopped

½ cup golden raisins

1 teaspoon salt

1. Warm the oil in a medium saucepan over medium heat. Add the mustard seeds and cumin seeds and cook, stirring constantly, until toasted, about 30 seconds.

2. Add the onion and cook, stirring occasionally, until soft, about 5 minutes. Stir in the ginger and turmeric and cook until just fragrant, about 2 minutes. Stir in the coriander and cardamom to combine.

3. Add the quince, ½ cup water, the vinegar, and brown sugar, and stir to combine. Bring to a simmer, cover, and cook, stirring once or twice, until tender, about 10 minutes. Stir in the apples, cover, and simmer until the apples are tender, about 10 minutes. Stir in the raisins and salt. Let cool to room temperature, then refrigerate in an airtight container for up to 2 weeks.

Extra Credit

- For an out-of-this-world **grilled cheese**, lacquer one side of the bread with this chutney, layer with thin-sliced ham, then cheddar, and toast in a skillet with lots of butter on both sides.

- Whisk 2 tablespoons of chutney with oil and vinegar; toss with chopped roasted root veggies like parsnips and carrots, spinach, pumpkin seeds, and pumpernickel croutons for a splendid **autumn salad**.

- The rarity of quince makes them perfect for a holiday table. Serve this chutney alongside **roast ham** or turkey instead of, or in addition to, cranberry sauce.

- For a sweet and savory side, top a baked **sweet potato** with this chutney, sour cream, and chopped bacon.

Toast with Raclette and Watercress

Preheat the oven to 400°F. Slice two ½-inch-thick slices from 1 loaf of rustic bread. Place the bread on a baking sheet in the oven until lightly toasted, 6 to 8 minutes. Transfer the toast to two plates.

Cut 5 ounces Raclette cheese into ½-inch cubes. In a medium cast-iron or nonstick skillet, heat the cheese cubes just until melted, then continue to cook, stirring once or twice, until the cheese starts to stick slightly to the bottom of the skillets and becomes melted and bubbly, about 8 minutes total.

Top both pieces of toast with some of the melted cheese, scraping up and including any sticky bits, and then top each serving with ¼ cup quince, apple, and turmeric chutney and a handful of watercress. Serve immediately. **Serves 2**

If you're a jammer, don't throw away the cores and peels of quince. They are packed with pectin. Freeze them so you can later simmer with water for a homemade pectin solution that will help firm up any number of preserves.

GRILLED ARTICHOKE TAPENADE

While tapenades are generally olive based, here olives are usurped by artichokes, which bring a similar umami flavor and meaty texture. This recipe is inspired by the artichokes at a special little place called Caputo's in Brooklyn. It was there I first encountered artichokes *sotto olio* (preserved in olive oil). As a California native I'd enjoyed artichokes my whole life, but I had never had anything like these: large bulbs grilled over a wood fire, partially blackened, and so deliciously smoky and earthy. This recipe uses frozen artichoke hearts which, when grilled, do a surprisingly good job of simulating the Caputo's experience and forming the basis for this flavor-packed, rustic sauce.

Makes about 2½ cups

1 (12-ounce) package frozen, thawed, and drained artichoke hearts

5 tablespoons extra-virgin olive oil

1 tablespoon plus 1 teaspoon fresh lemon juice

Sea salt and freshly ground black pepper

2 medium cloves garlic, finely chopped

1 tablespoon lemon zest

2 tablespoons drained capers

¼ cup chopped fresh flat-leaf parsley

1. Preheat a grill or grill pan to medium-high heat. In a medium bowl, toss the artichoke hearts with 2 tablespoons of the olive oil and 1 tablespoon of the lemon juice and season with ¼ teaspoon salt and ¼ teaspoon pepper. Working in batches if necessary, cook the artichokes on the grill, flipping them halfway through, until grill marks form on all sides, about 6 minutes total. Transfer to a large cutting board and, when cool enough to handle, coarsely chop and return to the bowl.

2. Warm the remaining 3 tablespoons olive oil and the garlic in a small skillet over medium heat. When the garlic begins to soften and is fragrant, stir in the lemon zest and capers. Pour the olive oil mixture over the artichokes. Stir in the parsley and remaining teaspoon of lemon juice. Season to taste with salt and pepper. Serve warm or room temperature. Store refrigerated in an airtight container for up to 1 week.

Extra Credit

• Stir the tapenade into brown rice, along with peas, fava beans, baby spinach, and radishes for a **spring rice salad**.

• Toss artichoke tapenade with **penne rigate**, chopped grilled chicken, and pea shoots; eat it warm or room temperature.

• Rub slices of grilled sourdough or rustic bread with raw garlic, then top with some of the tapenade for a quick and easy **bruschetta**.

• Create a breadless bruschetta for your gluten-free friends by spooning the tapenade into little romaine or butter **lettuce boats**.

Pan Bagnat

Slice four 4-inch-square ciabatta rolls in half crosswise. Tear out some of the soft bread from the inside of each half (save the scraps for bread crumbs or to feed the birds). Divide 2 drained 5-ounce cans tuna packed in olive oil among the bottom halves of each roll.

Top with thinly sliced seedless cucumber, thinly sliced tomatoes, thinly sliced red onion, and 4 thinly sliced hard-boiled eggs. Season to taste with salt and pepper. Then top with fresh basil leaves and the artichoke and lemon tapenade.

Wrap each sandwich tightly in plastic wrap and place them under something heavy, such as a heavy pot or cast-iron pan, until slightly pressed, about 30 minutes. Unwrap each sandwich and slice in half. Serve immediately or within 2 to 3 hours.
Serves 4

NIBLETY CORN RELISH

I've never been to the Deep South, but it's on my bucket list, primarily because of the food. When I lived in Brooklyn, I had a friend from New Orleans named Karina who taught me how to fry fish and cook okra. Corn relish is a traditional Southern condiment with sweet, vinegary qualities that cut through all that delicious, indulgent fried Southern fare. When developing this recipe, I played around with the proportions until I achieved my goal: a condiment that tastes like a sweet corn pickle. It is a great counterpoint to rich fried foods such as fried chicken or fish, as it adds a bright and tangy flavor that cuts through the grease. I even like eating it plain.

Makes about 2 cups

2 teaspoons canola oil

2 tablespoons finely chopped shallot

1½ teaspoons yellow mustard seeds

1 bay leaf

⅓ cup finely chopped red bell pepper

⅓ cup finely chopped green bell pepper

2 cups fresh shucked corn or thawed frozen corn

5 tablespoons white wine vinegar

3 tablespoons sugar

Sea salt

1. Heat the canola oil in a medium saucepan over medium heat. Add the shallot, mustard seeds, bay leaf, and red and green peppers. Cook, stirring occasionally, until the shallot has softened, about 4 minutes.

2. Add the corn and toss to combine. Add the vinegar and sugar and bring to a simmer, stirring occasionally. Season to taste with salt.

3. Let cool to room temperature, then discard the bay leaf. Use immediately or store refrigerated in an airtight container for up to 1 week.

Extra Credit

● Trick out a **lobster roll** with this relish instead of the usual butter and celery salt. Or add it to your arsenal of hot dog or sausage toppings.

● Spoon on top of **fried green tomatoes**.

● For a vintage-style appetizer, spread whipped cream **cheese on top of crackers** and top each with a small spoonful of niblety corn relish.

● Brighten up a pot of stewed **pinto beans** by using this sauce as a topper. In the Appalachians, this makes a fine supper along with a wedge of cornbread.

Cornmeal-Crusted Trout

Whisk 2 large eggs and ¼ cup whole milk in a large shallow dish. Season with 1¼ teaspoons salt and ½ teaspoon black pepper. In a separate shallow dish, combine 1¼ cups finely ground cornmeal with 1 teaspoon salt and ½ teaspoon black pepper.

Dip four 4-ounce boneless skin-on trout fillets into the egg mixture, then coat well on both sides in the cornmeal and place on a parchment-lined baking sheet.

Heat 3 tablespoons canola oil in a large cast-iron or heavy-bottomed skillet over medium-high heat. When hot, add the fillets in 2 batches if necessary and cook each batch until golden brown and crisp on both sides, 2 to 3 minutes per side. Transfer the fish to four plates and spoon the corn relish on top. Serve immediately. **Serves 4**

Confectionary

The Mother Ganache

Ganache is simply a fancy word for what you get when you stir chopped chocolate into hot heavy cream until the two come together. Its uses are endless. Warm, it can be drizzled onto cakes or ice cream, or used as a dunker for shortbread or biscotti. Cooled in the refrigerator, it can serve as a decadent spread on toast, used to fill cookie sandwiches, scooped to make a soft truffle filling, or even get whipped into a delectable chocolate frosting. Stir a few tablespoons into hot milk for instant fancy hot chocolate. Just make sure to buy the best-quality chocolate—I like Scharffen Berger or Callebaut—and equally good cream, since these ingredients are the stars.

Makes about 1 cup

4 ounces good-quality 62% semisweet chocolate

⅔ cup heavy cream

1 tablespoon unsalted butter, cut into small pieces

1. Use a large serrated knife to finely chop the chocolate and place it in a medium heatproof bowl.

2. Bring the cream just to a boil in a small saucepan over medium-high heat, 3 to 4 minutes, then turn off the heat. Pour the cream over the chocolate and let rest for 5 minutes.

3. Add the butter and stir until the butter is melted and the chocolate is smooth. Serve immediately or store refrigerated in an airtight container for up to 1 week. To reheat, bring the ganache to room temperature, then transfer to a large metal bowl and place on top of a pot of simmering water to create a double boiler. Stir until warm and smooth.

Mix It Up

Customize the mother sauce to your taste, and to use in different ways.

Passion Fruit Ganache

Substitute 4 ounces 70% bittersweet chocolate for the 62% semisweet chocolate. Stir in ¼ cup fresh passion fruit pulp with seeds (from 3 passion fruits) and 2 tablespoons passion fruit liqueur.

Aztec Ganache

Stir in ½ teaspoon chile powder, ½ teaspoon cinnamon, and 1 teaspoon pure vanilla extract.

Vegan Coconut & Almond Masala Ganache

Replace the cream with ⅔ cup full-fat coconut milk. Omit the butter and stir in ¼ cup smooth almond butter. Stir in ¾ teaspoon garam masala.

Salted Malted Ganache

Substitute 4 ounces milk chocolate for the 62% semisweet chocolate. Whisk ¼ cup malted milk powder into the hot heavy cream and stir in ½ teaspoon sea salt.

Extra Credit

• Peel a **banana**, freeze it on a stick, then dip into the passion fruit variation. Let it set until the chocolate is firm. A tropical paradise.

• Fold an equal amount of smooth **peanut butter** into the ganache and refrigerate until firm. Scoop out spoonfuls and roll into balls for a treat that's better than store-bought peanut butter cups.

• **Fondue** parties aren't just for cheese: Make it a dessert party with a big pot of this sauce, or better yet, one of each variation, along with a smorgasbord of fresh and dried fruits and biscotti for dipping.

QUÉBÉCOIS MAPLE BUTTER

When my husband first tried this sauce his eyes popped out of his head like a Warner Brothers cartoon character, and moments later, he was using his finger like a rubber scraper to frantically wipe up every molecule from the plate. Think of it as maple syrup on steroids—the butter, cream, and salt result in an alchemical concoction that tastes like liquefied maple sugar candy. Recommended for bears pre-hibernation, or anyone who could use some comfort against the cold.

Makes about 1 cup

¾ **cup pure maple syrup**

½ **cup heavy cream**

4 **tablespoons cold unsalted butter, cut into small pieces**

½ **teaspoon sea salt**

1. Bring the maple syrup and cream to a boil in a medium saucepan over medium-high heat, about 4 minutes. Continue to cook, stirring occasionally, until bubbling and slightly thickened, about 5 minutes.

2. Whisk in the butter and salt. Serve warm or room temperature. Store refrigerated in an airtight container for up to 2 weeks. Bring to room temperature or rewarm in a bowl set over a water bath.

Extra Credit

• For **cinnamon toast** fit for a queen, spread this maple butter on thick sourdough slices, let it sink in a minute, sprinkle with cinnamon, and bake until crispy at the edges.

• Pour over the top of a **Bundt cake** for instant icing.

• Revive day-old banana bread, **gingerbread**, or just about any quick bread by toasting slices then drizzling this sauce over the top.

• Pour over fresh-popped **popcorn** for a sweet-and-salty treat.

Cornmeal Crepes

In a high-powered blender, combine 1 cup all-purpose flour, ⅔ cup finely ground cornmeal, ½ teaspoon salt, 1 tablespoon sugar, 1¾ cups room-temperature whole milk, 2 large room-temperature eggs, and 3 tablespoon melted and cooled unsalted butter and blend until a smooth batter forms. (It should be the consistency of heavy cream.) Let it sit at room temperature for about 30 minutes.

In a small bowl, combine 2 tablespoons canola oil and 2 tablespoons melted unsalted butter. Heat an 8-inch crepe pan or heavy-bottomed skillet over high heat for about 2 minutes, until very hot,

turn off the heat and let sit for about 2 minutes. Then reheat the pan to medium and brush with some of the oil and butter mixture. Pour ¼ cup batter onto the pan and swirl to evenly coat.

Cook until bubbles form in the middle, about 2 minutes. Use a spatula to carefully flip the crepe over and continue to cook, about 1 minute more.

Transfer to a baking sheet or plate. Repeat the process until all the batter has been used. Divide among plates and drizzle with the Québécois maple butter. **Makes eleven 8-inch crepes**

MATCHA WHITE CHOCOLATE

I bought a tin of matcha (green tea powder) on a whim a while ago, in truth because the packaging was so pretty. Naturally, it sat in the cupboard untouched for months. I finally decided to do something about the lonely container and thus was born Matcha White Chocolate. Think of the silky texture of chocolate sauce, but much more delicately flavored with (and tinted by) green tea. Creamy and comforting, this pourable sauce might also be even a tiny bit healthy due to the green tea (just humor me). A jar of this sauce makes a great hostess present; the pale jade color invariably elicits oohs and aahs. In fact I think it may even be prettier than that original tin.

Makes about 1¼ cups

4 ounces white chocolate

1 cup heavy cream

2 teaspoons matcha powder

Pinch of sea salt

1. Finely chop the white chocolate and place in a medium bowl.

2. Whisk the cream and matcha powder in a small saucepan until combined. Over medium heat, bring to a simmer, about 4 minutes. Begin whisking again as the mixture comes to a boil and continue until it is very smooth, about 2 minutes.

3. Pour the hot matcha cream over the chocolate. Let sit for about 5 minutes. Whisk until smooth, then whisk in a pinch of salt. Use warm or at room temperature.

Extra Credit

• Top a bowl of berries with a scoop of vanilla **ice cream** and drizzle with this sauce for a colorful variation on a summer sundae.

• Transform a plain bakery-bought **cheesecake** into something spectacular by spreading a thin layer of this sauce on top.

• Stir into **rice pudding** and sprinkle more matcha on top.

• How about a symphony in green? Serve over **pistachio cake** and garnish with mint leaves.

Matchaccino

In a medium saucepan, warm 1 cup whole milk and 1½ cups evaporated milk over medium heat until just simmering, about 8 minutes.

Transfer the milk mixture to a high-powered blender along with 1 batch warm matcha white chocolate and blend until frothy, about 2 minutes.

Pour into mugs and serve garnished with fresh whipped cream and a sprinkle of matcha powder, if desired. **Serves 4**

KATIA'S CREAMY VANILLA ELIXIR

I developed this custard sauce, similar to a crème anglaise, in honor of our daughter, Katia. She will eat anything, just as long as it is white. While I can count the meals she will tolerate on one hand, she loves to help me in the kitchen, and I always reward her by putting a little pure vanilla extract on her wrists like perfume. Hence Katia's Creamy Vanilla Elixir: warm, creamy, and sweet with lots of vanilla flavor (and free of any colors that might distract your palate). This sauce is a puffy cloud of pure comfort. Serve with warm chocolate anything, from cake to soufflé—for that matter, drizzle it on most any dessert. But if you're serving it to fancy company, take care not to lick the spoon.

Makes about 2 cups

1 vanilla bean

½ cup whole milk

1½ cups heavy cream

2 large egg yolks

¼ cup sugar

1 teaspoon cornstarch

1 tablespoon cold unsalted butter, cut into small pieces

1 teaspoon pure vanilla extract

Pinch of sea salt

1. Use a sharp knife to make a vertical slit down the length of the vanilla bean and place it in a medium saucepan along with the milk and cream. Bring to a simmer over medium-low heat, stirring occasionally, 12 to 15 minutes.

2. Meanwhile, whisk together the egg yolks, sugar, and cornstarch in a medium bowl until pale yellow and smooth but thick.

3. Slowly pour the cream mixture, a ladleful at a time, into the egg yolk mixture while whisking constantly to temper the egg yolks.

4. Pour the mixture back into the saucepan and continue to cook over medium heat, stirring constantly until simmering and thickened, 8 to 10 minutes. Turn off the heat and whisk in the butter, vanilla, and salt.

5. Pour the sauce through a fine-mesh sieve into a clean medium bowl and let cool slightly. Serve warm or place plastic wrap directly on the surface of the sauce to prevent a skin from forming and refrigerate until cool. At this point, you may transfer to an airtight container and store, refrigerated, for up to 3 days.

Extra Credit

● Serve **angel food cake** or pound cake and fresh berries over a pool of Katia's creamy vanilla elixir.

● Blend with milk, bananas, and ice cubes for a thick and creamy milkshake. This is great if you want a **milkshake** but don't have ice cream around.

● For grown-ups only: blend the elixir with whole milk, nutmeg, and rum for a riff on **eggnog**.

● Drizzle on **pears** poached in wine sauce.

Pear, Apple, and Cardamom Tart

Thaw 1 sheet from a 17.3-ounce package puff pastry according to package instructions. Lightly sprinkle a countertop with all-purpose flour and place the puff pastry on top. Lightly flour the pastry and roll it out into a 12- by 14-inch rectangle. Transfer to a parchment-lined baking sheet and place in the refrigerator for about 15 minutes to firm up. Preheat the oven to 400°F.

Peel 2 Golden Delicious apples and 2 ripe but firm Bosc pears. Use a sharp knife to thinly slice them into ¼-inch-thick slices. Place the apples in one medium bowl and the pears in another. Toss each with 1 teaspoon fresh lemon juice, 1½ tablespoons sugar, ¼ teaspoon ground cardamom, and a pinch of salt.

Alternating pear and apple, arrange the fruit slices close together and overlapping in four rows on top of the dough, leaving a 1-inch border around the edges. Dot the fruit with 1 tablespoon butter cut into small pieces.

Fold the edges in over the fruit to create a ½-inch dough rim. Pinch the four corners to seal the dough. In a small bowl, beat 1 tablespoon water with 1 egg. Brush the egg wash on the rim and sprinkle the rim with 1 tablespoon sugar.

Bake until the puff pastry is deep golden brown and the fruit is cooked, 35 to 40 minutes. Let cool slightly before slicing the tart into 8 slices. Serve warm or room temperature drizzled with the vanilla elixir. **Makes one 12- by 14-inch tart; serves 8**

COCONUT AND LEMONGRASS INFUSION

Lemongrass is a long and stalky perennial herb usually grown in warm and tropical climates. Originally from India but used with great frequency in Southeast Asian cooking, it has a lovely, distinctive, fresh, zingy aroma. Being quite fibrous, it is best to think of lemongrass not so much as an ingredient to use raw on its own, but as an herb that flavors something else. This can be achieved either by finely chopping the less fibrous part and adding it to a dish, or by steeping it in water or a syrup to create an infusion, as is done here. This recipe combines the bright notes of lemongrass with the richness of coconut milk. The result is a sauce that allows you to make over a wide range of desserts, such as the kebabs opposite, with an exotic and tropical flavor profile.

Makes about 1⅓ cups

4 stalks fresh lemongrass

¼ cup sugar

½ cup full-fat coconut milk

½ cup sweetened condensed milk

2 tablespoons fresh lime juice

2 teaspoons lime zest

¼ teaspoon sea salt

1. Tear off any dried outer leaves from the lemongrass, cut off the stem ends, and finely chop. You should have about ¾ cup. Combine the chopped lemongrass, sugar, and ¼ cup water in a medium saucepan. Bring to a boil over medium heat, stirring until the sugar has dissolved. Turn off the heat, cover the pan, and steep until the syrup is very fragrant, about 1 hour.

2. Pour the mixture through a fine-mesh sieve into a medium bowl. Whisk in the coconut milk, sweetened condensed milk, lime juice, lime zest, and salt. The sauce will keep in an airtight container in the refrigerator for up to 1 week.

Extra Credit

• For a party, wow your guests with a batch of **piña coladas** with this as an optional stir-in.

• Blend the sauce with vanilla ice cream and a shot of orange juice for a **shake** that tastes like a Creamsicle on an island vacation.

• Make a tropical **trifle**. Chop up bananas and pineapple. Layer in a clear glass dish with cut-up ladyfingers, whipped cream, and drizzles of the lemongrass infusion.

• Dip **shortbread** cookies into the sauce and top with toasted coconut flakes.

Grilled Fruit and Cake Kebabs

Peel and cut 1 ripe but firm mango, half of a peeled and cored pineapple, and 4 peeled kiwis into 1½-inch chunks. In a medium bowl, toss the fruit with 2 tablespoons sugar and 2 teaspoons lime zest.

Alternately thread the chunks of fruit and 4 cups cubed angel food or pound cake (store-bought is okay) onto eight 10-inch skewers. Reserve any excess syrup in the bowl.

Preheat a grill or grill pan over medium heat. Lightly oil the grill and cook the kebabs, turning occasionally, until grill marks form on all sides, 3 to 5 minutes total. Transfer to a serving platter. Drizzle any reserved syrup over the skewers. Serve with a ramekin of coconut and lemongrass infusion for dipping. **Serves 4**

Big sections of lemongrass stalks often get discarded because they are too woody and tough to chop. Try making lemongrass tea instead, by steeping them in boiling water until the flavor is released. (This is also a good way to use up leftover fresh ginger.)

BLUEBERRY, LEMON, AND THYME COMPOTE

Trivia question: what's the difference between a compote and a coulis? If you said a compote is made of fruit cut into chunks and cooked in a syrup and other flavorings, whereas a coulis usually describes a strained and smooth fruit purée, you're "berry" correct! (If you enjoyed that, book me now for your wedding or corporate event—I'll even come dressed as a berry of your choice.)

Moving on . . . in this recipe, I've gone the compote route, since I love the texture of whole berries within the sauce. (Bonus: you don't have to mess with a strainer.) A hint of fresh thyme and the zing of lemon further livens up the proceedings. Besides using it on sweet things, try this compote as a finishing touch over roast lamb. I know that sounds crazy, but trust me, it's phenomenal.

Makes about 1¼ cups

¼ cup sugar

1 teaspoon cornstarch

1 teaspoon lemon zest

1½ cups fresh or frozen thawed blueberries

3 sprigs fresh thyme

1 tablespoon fresh lemon juice

1. In a medium saucepan, whisk together the sugar, cornstarch, lemon zest, and ¼ cup water until the sugar dissolves.

2. Add the blueberries and thyme sprigs. Bring to a simmer over medium heat and cook until slightly thickened, stirring occasionally, about 8 minutes total. Stir in the lemon juice. Let cool to room temperature and remove the thyme sprigs. Use immediately or store refrigerated in an airtight container for up to 1 week or freeze for up to 3 months.

Extra Credit

● Instead of PB and J, spread a fancy nut butter such as almond or hazelnut on **whole-grain toast** and top with the blueberry, lemon, and thyme compote.

● Make a lemon blueberry **Eton mess**. Fold some compote into whipped cream. Add crushed meringue and fold it in. Divide among cups and serve with a sprig of mint.

● Cornbread slices or **corn muffins** leftover from dinner? Upcycle them for breakfast the next day by toasting them, spreading with cream cheese or Greek yogurt, then topping with this compote.

● Toss this compote with **sliced peaches** for a fruit salad that puts the canned stuff to shame.

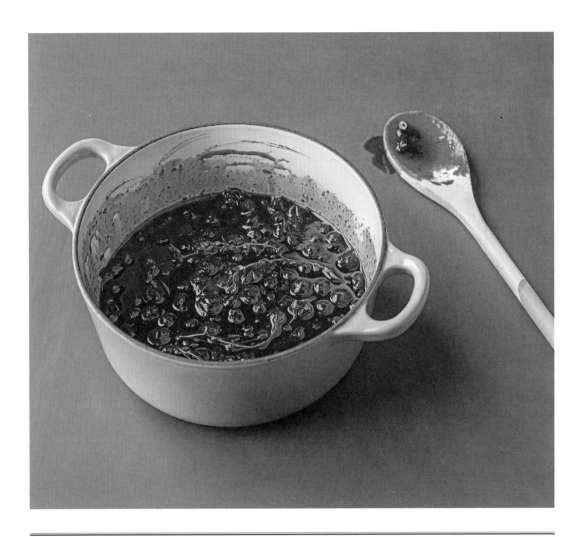

Lemon Ginger Posset

In a medium saucepan, whisk together ½ cup plus 1 tablespoon sugar, 1 teaspoon lemon zest, and 2½ teaspoons freshly grated ginger.

Stir in 1¾ cups heavy cream and bring the mixture to a boil over medium-high heat. Continue to boil, stirring occasionally, for about 5 minutes. Remove from the heat and stir in ⅓ cup fresh lemon juice; let cool for 15 minutes.

Stir the cream mixture again and pour it through a fine-mesh sieve into a large measuring cup. Divide the mixture among four ramekins or jars. Refrigerate until set, at least 4 hours or overnight. Serve the posset topped with some blueberry, lemon, and thyme compote and a sprig of fresh thyme on each portion. **Serves 4**

SECRET INGREDIENT CARAMEL

When the weather turns cold every year, I get the caramel-making bug. Watching plain sugar transform into such a sublime confection has always fascinated me—it feels like a magic trick. It's a good thing too that I like to watch closely because caramel can go from just right to burnt in a moment. You must remain by the stove with eyes glued on the pot. Like many other people out there, I love salt in my caramel, but I wanted to develop something beyond the ubiquitous sea salt variety. The umami found in miso and soy sauce totally fits the bill. Sounds a bit funky, I know, but just give it a try and you'll see. An added bonus: this sauce makes a great gift presented in a jar to family and friends.

Makes about 1¾ cups

1 cup heavy cream

3 tablespoons sweet white miso

1 cup sugar

¼ cup golden syrup, or light corn syrup

¼ cup (½ stick) unsalted butter, cut into small pieces

1 teaspoon low-sodium soy sauce

1. Warm the cream in a small saucepan over medium-low heat until hot but not boiling, about 5 minutes. Add the miso and whisk until smooth. Keep warm over low heat.

2. In a medium saucepan, stir together the sugar, golden syrup, and ¼ cup water. Dip a brush in water and brush it around the rim of the pan to wash away any sugar crystals. Heat over medium heat without stirring until the sugar has dissolved and becomes a medium amber color, 12 to 15 minutes.

3. Whisk in the cream mixture; add gradually as it will bubble up the sides of the saucepan. Cook until slightly thickened, about 3 minutes. With the heat off, whisk in the butter and soy sauce until smooth. Serve warm or room temperature. Store refrigerated in an airtight container for up to 2 weeks. Rewarm in a large bowl over a simmering pot of water.

Extra Credit

- Drizzle cooled caramel over a vanilla pound cake, or even **chocolate cake**, or serve a slice of cake in a pool of caramel.

- Draw zigzag lines with a spoonful of caramel over **crepes**, waffles, or pancakes to transform them into an instant dessert.

- Goose up **apple pie** with this caramel sauce for the holidays; the secret ingredient will get the whole table talking.

- Roast **pineapple** rings, place on a serving plate, and spoon this sauce into the hole in the middle.

Godzilla Sundae

Place 2 tablespoons of the caramel sauce in the bottom of each of two parfait glasses. Top each with a large scoop of vanilla ice cream drizzled with another tablespoon of caramel. Sprinkle 1 tablespoon dried salted edamame and ¼ teaspoon black sesame seeds on top of the caramel. Then top with 2 tablespoons chopped strawberries.

Repeat with 1 more large scoop of ice cream, more caramel, dried edamame, black sesame seeds, and strawberries.

Top with a large dollop of fresh whipped cream and sprinkles of dried salted edamame and sesame seeds. Serve immediately. **Serves 4**

The keys to making a smooth and creamy caramel are a) melting and then b) caramelizing the sugar—without crystals forming at any point. This is why many recipes instruct you to brush the edges of the saucepan with water to remove sugar crystals.

HONEY BEAR NUT SYRUP

Syrupy, nutty, and a little spicy, this sauce is inspired by the many flavors of Sicily and its Mediterranean-Arab cuisine, which boasts influences from Italy, Greece, Spain, France, and the Mideast. The fennel seeds and orange freshen the palate, while the subtle, rich, nutty flavors of pistachio and sesame add body and crunch. A lot of concentrated flavors are packed into this sauce, so a little goes a long way. The sweet-and-savory combination works well as a component to a cheese plate or drizzled over grilled fresh figs, peaches, and/or apricots.

Makes about 1 cup

¼ cup raw unsalted pistachios

¼ cup raw unsalted almonds

½ teaspoon fennel seeds

1 tablespoon raw sesame seeds

⅓ cup extra-virgin olive oil

6 tablespoons honey

1 teaspoon orange zest

¼ teaspoon sea salt

Pinch of freshly ground black pepper

1. Preheat the oven to 400°F. Scatter the nuts on a baking sheet and bake for 6 to 8 minutes, stirring once halfway through, until lightly toasted. Transfer to a cutting board to cool slightly. Finely chop the nuts.

2. Place the fennel seeds and sesame seeds in a small skillet over medium heat and stir constantly until toasted, 3 to 4 minutes. Immediately transfer the seeds to a small bowl.

3. In a medium saucepan, heat the olive oil over medium heat, about 2 minutes. Add the honey and stir until smooth. Add the reserved nuts and seeds and stir to combine and heat through. Stir in the orange zest, salt, and black pepper. Serve warm or room temperature. Store in an airtight container at room temperature for up to 1 week. Stir well before using the sauce, as the ingredients separate overnight.

Extra Credit

● Grill a piece of anadama, banana, or **zucchini bread**, then spread with crème fraîche and drizzle with the honey nut syrup.

● Add mustard and vinegar to the sauce to make a salad dressing—works especially well with spicy, nutty greens or **chicories** (e.g., arugula, spinach, dandelion greens, or radicchio).

● Use as a glaze for steamed, mashed, or roasted carrots, **parsnips**, turnips, or rutabaga.

● Serve **steel-cut oats** with almond milk, dried cranberries, and a drizzle of this syrup.

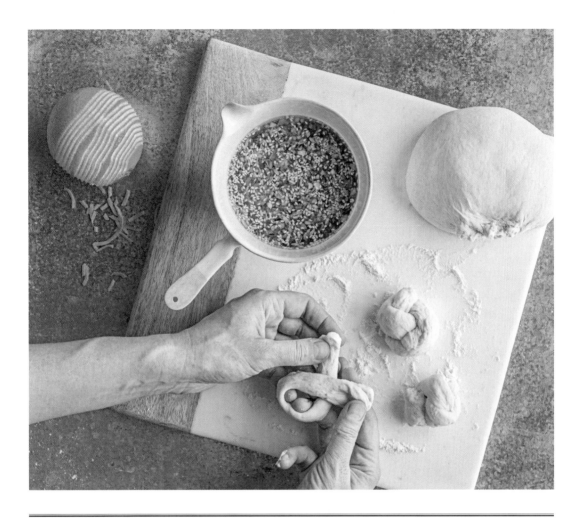

Sticky Bread Knots

Preheat the oven to 475°F. Divide 1 pound pizza dough into 12 pieces and roll each piece between your hands into a 6-inch rope. Form each into a knot by crossing the rope ends, leaving a hole in the center. Bring the end that lies on top up through the bottom of the hole. You may have to tug on the end a bit to get it to come through.

Place the knots 2 inches apart on a parchment-lined baking sheet. Brush each with olive oil and sprinkle with salt. Bake until golden brown on top, 12 to 14 minutes.

Place the honey bear nut syrup in a shallow bowl. When the knots are done, transfer the parchment paper, with the knots, to a countertop. Immediately roll each knot in the honey syrup to coat and spoon some additional nuts and sauce over the top. Allow to cool and firm up. Serve warm or room temperature. **Makes 12**

Sauce-Making Tools

In my cooking classes, I occasionally get asked about what tools and supplies I would recommend when setting up a home kitchen. I could go on and on about this, but for the purposes of this book let me stick with sauces. The following are my go-to devices and tools for sauce-making.

High-Powered Blender

After having gone through many blenders over the years I am convinced that investing in a good one will save you money in the long run. Even the mid-priced ones tend to break down. The high-powered blenders, on the other hand, are workhorses that can take a good beating (no pun intended). A high-powered blender also yields the most velvety sauce. Make sure your blender has a clear pitcher; you need to be able to see the texture of your mixture to know when you've reached the desired consistency.

Immersion Blender

While it won't achieve quite the same smoothness as a high-powered blender, an immersion blender is a good option if you are making large quantities of sauce in a heavy pot or blended soups. They are generally easier to clean and take up less space—both definite bonuses.

Food Processor

For chopping and coarsely blending ingredients, nothing beats a food processor. It gives you more control than a blender; the pulse function is especially useful for this purpose. I also love that you can clean most food processor parts in a dishwasher.

Mortar and Pestle

It's physically more work, but grinding spices and herbs by hand with a mortar and pestle not only allows you to release their fragrant oils but also gives you total control over the grind. (Plus they look so pretty on the countertop. You can collect beautiful specimens from around the world: volcanic stone from Mexico, marble from Italy, olive wood from Spain.)

Fine-Mesh Strainer

I can't say enough good things about these tools. I've used them to help get optimal smoothness in so many mixtures—including getting lumps, seeds, and citrus peel out of sauces. If your sauce is thick and won't strain easily, using a rubber spatula to push it through the fine mesh usually does the trick.

Rubber Spatula

The silicone variety is dishwasher safe and great for getting into the corners of a saucepan that a wooden or metal spoon can't reach. Use them to scrape every last bit of sauce out of the saucepan or bowl and into the serving dish.

Large Wooden and Metal Spoons

Use heavy wooden spoons when making creamy sauces such as the Katia's Creamy Vanilla Elixir (page 154) since they are thicker than a metal spoon and can really smooth and stir the thick sauce. I prefer metal spoons for sauces that are quite hot in temperature and thinner in texture.

Heavy-Bottomed Pots and Pans

Good-quality pots and pans are always wise investments. The heavy bottoms help with even heating. The ones I use are stainless steel. For sauce-making purposes I recommend having on hand a small saucepan, medium saucepan, large saucepan, and a large high-sided skillet.

Dutch Oven

This is great when making a larger batch of sauce. I like how the mixture heats up slowly and evenly.

Cast-Iron Skillet

I got rid of my nonstick pans years ago and don't miss them at all. My seasoned cast iron skillet has replaced the need for nonstick. Cooking on it feels so much safer, plus it wasn't too expensive and will last a lifetime. Just make sure you keep the surface well seasoned. I tend to use soap very sparingly on these skillets—only when really needed. Normally all they need is a good scrub with coarse salt and water. After cleaning, place the wet skillet back on the burner until dry, then use a paper towel or rag to rub with a thin coating of a neutral oil such as canola.

Cast-Iron Stovetop Grill

We sometimes grill outside in the winter, but that's not always fun in Maine. When feeling less ambitious we take it indoors with this handy pan. A cast-iron stovetop grill allows you to make some of the grilled sauces such as the Artichoke and Lemon Tapenade (page 142) and the Eggplant Zhoug (page 120) inside. Clean and season the grill pan the same way you would a cast-iron skillet (see opposite).

Microplane

These tools work like a box grater, but are way less bulky and can fit in the drawer. Consequently I have them in every shape and size. I use them for grating cheese, citrus peel, chocolate, cinnamon, and nutmeg.

Reamer or Citrus Juicer

If you use a lot of fresh citrus in your cooking, a good reamer or citrus juicer is a must. You can always use your hands to squeeze the fresh fruit, but on the East Coast of the U.S., where citrus is pricier, you want to make sure to get every last drop of juice out of the fruit.

Whisk

A good stainless-steel whisk smooths out and lightens the texture of sauces. It's the classic symbol of a saucier, and for good reason.

Acknowledgments

Developing, writing, and styling the recipes for this book has been a thrill. It also has been a massive undertaking that truly took a village to accomplish. I would like to give my thanks to the following:

First and foremost, to my wonderful family and friends for their patience, love, feedback, and encouragement throughout this process.

To my husband, Jon, for your love and endless support, for making me laugh, and for your keen editorial eye and unpaid late night/early morning editing.

To my Relish&Co. friends and partners, Stacey Cramp and Jennifer S. Muller, for your fabulous visual/design sense and talent. Not a day goes by that I don't feel grateful and lucky that we found each other and get to work together.

To Kyle Books for giving me this extraordinary opportunity.

To Chris Steighner, editor, for your advice, ideas, and superb editing skills. And to Sarah Scheffel, whose copyedits greatly improved the text throughout.

To Heather Noonan-Kelly, whose photo-editing talent and on-set assistance with both photos and food prep made our shoots run more smoothly.

To all the recipe testers, whose feedback helped me tweak, refine, and improve these sauces and dishes: Gillian Kitchings, Moire Madden, Linda Christman, Melissa Lacasse, and to my two Relish&Co. partners.

Thank you to Anwar and Shaymaa Jailawi for your invaluable child care help, friendship, and feedback as recipe tasters.

To the Institute of Culinary Education for the skills, techniques, and knowledge that laid the foundation of my culinary journey, and to all the teachers, mentors, and colleagues I've learned from along the way.

About the Author

Vanessa Seder is a chef, food stylist, teacher, and a founding member of Relish&Co., a culinary design collaborative based in Portland, Maine. A graduate of the Institute of Culinary Education, Vanessa has developed recipes for *Ladies Home Journal*, *Real Simple*, *All You*, *Health*, *Cooking Light*, and Hannaford's *Fresh*. Previously an associate food editor at *Ladies Home Journal*, Vanessa has also worked as a food stylist for television, video, magazines, and books, as well as for national brands. She is also a regular culinary instructor at the Stonewall Kitchen headquarters in York, Maine.